WISDOM FACTORIES

AI, GAMES, AND THE EDUCATION OF A MODERN WORKER

TIM DASEY, PH.D.

Published in the United States by Rejuvenate Publishing, Massachusetts.

Wisdom Factories was written without AI help except for the ChatGPT excerpt in Chapter 1.

Paperback ISBN: 979-8-9882386-0-7
Hardcover ISBN: 979-8-9882386-2-1
eBook ISBN: 979-8-9882386-1-4

Dedication

For my children Julia and Rachel—they're wise beyond their years, inspire me every day, and are the best teachers I've ever had.

CONTENTS

PROLOGUE

*The saddest aspect of life right now is that science gathers
knowledge faster than society gathers wisdom.*

Isaac Asimov[1]

Many of you have seen the video, and if you're like me you fell for it. Before watching it, you're told to count the number of times a small group of adults pass a basketball to one another. Afterward you're asked whether you saw the gorilla. In that same video, a person dressed in a gorilla suit walks into the midst of the ball-passers, thumps its chest a few times, and moseys out of the scene. I never saw the gorilla. I was too busy counting passes.

It's called inattentional blindness.[2,3] It refers to a human weakness in noticing even obvious things when our attention is elsewhere.

Wisdom Factories is pointing out inattentional blindness in education. Debates rage about parental control of learning content, inequality of schooling opportunity, teenage mental health, etc. Those are big issues, but I think we're not paying attention to the gorilla.

The core fundamentals of schooling should be in question, yet few are talking about that. The other issues are significant, but they're premised on the assumption of tweaking the existing model. What if teaching detailed knowledge isn't the right objective? Then arguing about those particulars is beside the point. What if we achieve equality, but everyone is headed in the wrong direction? Then we're just equally off-course. What if student mental health problems are partly a symptom of school pressure and classroom mismatches with the real world? Then the way to help is to examine the model.

The impetus for fundamental reorientation of school is technology—especially Artificial Intelligence (AI). I've worked in AI for over three decades, most of it at MIT Lincoln Laboratory. I felt a growing urgency about school's mismatch with an AI world...well before the emergence of eerily human-like AI chatbots or image generators. AI is capable of a ton of traditionally human tasks, and its scope of impact keeps growing.

The big issue isn't student cheating or figuring out how to use AI in the classroom; it's that the work that AI is grabbing is the same as schooling's focus. Students are set up to compete with AI rather than collaborate with it. They'll lose that competition.

There is understandable focus on AI's warts and potential misuses, but people are largely ignoring the other side of the equation. Workers need different cognitive skills to complement AI. Humanity needs to evolve too.

I had my first epiphany about five years ago when I learned about progress in an AI sub-field called AutoML (Automated Machine Learning). AutoML tries to automate major aspects of an AI developer's job. It is AI that builds AI. I learned it was already doing better than human designers. I realized then that Science, Technology, Engineering, and Math (STEM) skills...while undeniably important...are not going to ensure job safety.

The story has long been that as software, AI, and other technologies permeate more jobs, it will be knowledge of those tools that will preserve or amplify a worker's value. AutoML tears that story apart. If the top rung of technical workers can be automated (AI developers command huge salaries), then so can most of the detailed work in any profession. Automation risk is independent of our academic dividing lines. Getting workers to be technically savvy is helpful, but it isn't a panacea. All detailed, knowledge-oriented work is at risk of being significantly augmented—if not replaced—by AI.

AI is gobbling *expertise*—the core purpose of conventional schooling. People will be responsible for the vaguer, big-picture intellectual cousin—*wisdom*. Long sought but mostly unrealized learning goals like critical thinking, relationship skills, and creativity can no longer be add-ons. We must design schools so they are the top priorities.

Schools are expertise factories, but we need wisdom factories. Whether we can make that change will determine how many can enjoy the fruits of AI instead of being trampled by it.

My second epiphany was a creeping realization driven by major differences in the cognitive underpinnings of wisdom and expertise. They aren't just learned differently; learning wisdom is upside down from the expertise paradigm. I realized schools can't get to a wisdom focus by pasting those priorities on top of an expertise model. A fundamental paradigm shift is required. We can't easily get there from here.

Wisdom is learned through experience. In particular, it comes from varied experiences on complex, multidisciplinary challenges that have no predefined answer or unclear problem statements. Those experiences fuel abstract and domain-transcendent concepts. The wise tend toward adaptable, jack-of-all-trades types instead of niche performers. Unfortunately, most schooling still prioritizes delivery of lots of detail from within disciplinary silos.

The experiential learning requirement exposes another challenge. Experience with complex, big-picture challenges doesn't grow on trees. Many people have few such experiences in real life, and if they do, it takes a long time. That's why wisdom is associated with the aged. Apprenticeships, case studies, and extended-duration, open-ended projects can help, but they are time consuming and expose learners to a limited variety of situations. Wisdom needs lots of variety across situational contexts and application domains to create the abstract concepts that drive it.

How can we accelerate wisdom-fueling experience? I already had a tool in mind. For over a decade, my teams developed games to study how workers make decisions and what technologies might help them. The lessons were broader than how to apply AI to work. I learned games are an incredibly versatile tool for teaching abstract concepts and processes that fuel wisdom. Learners can be exposed to more situations and can fail on the way to competence without bad life consequences. Games are experience accelerants.

Wisdom Factories explores a dramatically different paradigm for educating modern workers. The first three chapters describe what AI and the changing nature of the world is doing to work, and outline why wisdom is the safe room. Chapter 1 discusses AI's work task consumption, while Chapter 2 describes the wisdom-oriented roles that remain and the personal characteristics that accompany the wise. Chapter 3 explains how the need for human wisdom derives from the high complexity of the modern problems we face...in addition to automation. The middle chapters discuss the cognitive underpinnings of wisdom (Chapter 4) and how experience and reflection drive its learning (Chapter 5). The last four chapters discuss solution aspects. Chapter 6 talks about the power of gaming. Chapter 7 is about how learning wisdom requires an educational model that's upside down from conventional ones. Chapter 8 discusses a process I call Productivity Therapy that will be important for managing AI. Finally, Chapter 9 recommends first steps in this massive wisdom reorientation.

The businesses and societies that can enhance the wisdom of their people...and prove they have...will be at a huge competitive advantage. Those first movers and their AI partners will have a leg up on solving the world's most difficult problems.

It has long been true that the foundation of prosperity is education. It still is, but I worry its relevance is rapidly shrinking. AI is advancing dramatically, and there's no end in sight to that improvement. People and institutions evolve slowly. This is a crisis that demands great urgency.

My goal is to start a conversation that we seem to be avoiding, drowned out by concerns of automation's veracity, bias, or other shortcomings.

We need to talk about humanity's evolution, too.

1.

AI'S EXPERTISE TAKEOVER

Rapid and accelerating digitization is likely to bring economic rather than environmental disruption, stemming from the fact that as computers get more powerful, companies have less need for some kinds of workers. Technological progress is going to leave behind some people, perhaps even a lot of people, as it races ahead.

Andrew McAfee and Erik Brynjolfsson[4]

Micromanagement lobotomizes, and brains fight back. That's where Ned Ludlam had gotten. "Square the needles" was his father's latest complaint. Ned picked up a hammer and destroyed the textile machine.[5]

A few decades later, in the 1810s, Ned was a wanted man. The English government suspected him of orchestrating textile machine destruction. By then "Ludd" was his moniker. Ned never admitted to the deeds, but when machines were sabotaged people would quip "Ned Ludd did it."[6] "Captain" or "King Ludd" was his taunting title for the police. Several times the authorities thought they had closed in on their man only to hear rumors of him somewhere else. Many thought he lived in Sherwood Forest—home of Robin Hood centuries earlier.

The authorities never found Ned, but we reference him today. He was either complete fiction or distinct from the legend.[7] His follow-ers—the Luddites—weren't made up. They were deemed a threat to public order. It became a capital offense to destroy a textile machine.

Machine sabotage still occurs.[8] In the late 80s, I had a part-time job maintaining a security robot in a large corporate warehouse. One service call was especially memorable. The robot's R2D2-style head was broken at the neck. It was no accident. (The perpetrator was no Mensa candidate either; the robot head was a camera!) Some modern-day cyberattacks also aim for destruction, payback, or protest.

The term Luddite can now be a slur. It can refer to technophobes like those who couldn't work the VCR in the 1990s, the DVR in the 2000s, or the smartphone settings now. More often the term alludes to paranoia about technology and what it will bring. Luddites are especially worried about job loss.

Many workers worry about technology affecting their own jobs. According to a 2019 survey of about 8,000 employees, roughly one in four workers believed technology would threaten their job in the next five years.[9]

Are the Luddites wrong to fear technology[10], or are we headed for the dawn of new industries with way more jobs than before? Will many boats sink, or will the tide lift all?

Economists call the belief that technology will kill jobs the "Luddite Fallacy." Time and again, their analyses show more net jobs result from automation. Jobs can be lost as technology improves production efficiency, but it also can increase consumption by lowering prices, improving quality, or doing something else customers want. People buy more and *voila*—more jobs! New technologies also need people to design, build, market, and sell them. Whatever the technology, "don't worry about it" is the vibe many economists give. They have a lot of history to back that up.

I can clearly imagine that someday AI and the other machines it produces could do everything that any human being could do. It's not going to happen within the seeable future, but brains are proof that it can be done. The question is when we will get close enough to that point that long-held economic principles like the Luddite Fallacy are stretched beyond their validity.

We're not even remotely close to that level of AI sophistication. AI may appear to understand something...but it doesn't. There are still plenty of talents that people can have that AI does not. The advances in AI are coming shockingly quickly, but right now it can be thought of as a reflex that responds to patterns of information with another pattern of information. It doesn't think, and despite lots of work to get it to do so, there's apparently a long way to go. It will take paradigm shifts in the technology to rival all aspects of human cognition, and we stink at forecasting the timing of those advancements.

It's not job loss *per se* that concerns me. Despite my reflex analogy, AI cannot be shrugged off anymore. It's a huge deal—a sweeping suite of advancements akin to the steam engine, electricity, and computers in terms of impact. Many, many workers will need to evolve or move to another form of work...if they can. The more salient concern is whether people will be capable of the new work, and whether those roles can offer them a good standard of living. That's where I'm worried. The Luddite Fallacy doesn't say the transition will be painless.

I argue that existing school paradigms will not get workers the skills they need for the AI era. Before I get to that story, I need to flesh out the challenges. These frame the educational needs.

The first three chapters discuss AI, the evolving nature of work, and the human skills that are demanded of this era.

I begin in this chapter by describing AI's impact on work. Whether or not your job remains when the dust settles, I am confident that most work will change enormously. Moreover, it will change quickly—over years, not decades—given both a stunning pace of technical advance and the human creativity in using AI.

I'm not going to claim the Luddite Fallacy will be broken. A forecast of mass unemployment isn't necessary. Job changes are enough to concern me. We're in for quite a ride!

THE EVOLUTION OF AI

Discussing AI is fraught with complications. It is frequently described in too much detail for most audiences, or at a philosophical level that lacks the concreteness needed to understand its specific impacts. It's highly complicated technology, both in design and behavior, so it has many facets. It can feel like there are no consistent answers to reasonable questions.

So let me put aside a few potential distractions from the get-go.

I'm not going to teach you how AI works. That's a complex subject for other books.

I'm not going to get into the philosophical debates.

Is AI really intelligent? I don't know how to begin that conversation. Are people intelligent? Are children? If we agree on the answer, does it change what AI will do?

Will it become conscious and control our lives or go all *Matrix* on us? Nobody can see that far ahead. That will require many advances in the technology, and perhaps humanity will apply the brakes in time. Anyway, I limit my futurism to the seeable horizon and not beyond it.

Whether AI will take your job, change it enough to make you irrelevant, or perhaps change the passion you have toward the transformed version, is a person- and job-specific question.

I can say only a few overarching things with high certainty. AI is on the way to doing a ton of tasks as well or better than people. It'll replace many high-expertise tasks as well as low-skill ones. It'll affect every job.

High certainty? Really? If you've been following its progress, you'll know that AI has been overhyped many times.

The early computer pioneer Alan Turing (whose fame resurged after the 2014 movie *The Imitation Game*) presumed in the 1940s that once machines could think, it would be only a matter of time before they exceeded human capabilities.[11] That promise, oft promoted in the intervening decades, has been partially fulfilled. AI can already do many tasks better than people, including some that society has lauded as intellectual pinnacles. It just doesn't think.

The AI path has had many dead ends and premature celebrations.

Early attempts in the 50s through 70s tried to capture human judgment with rule sets, resulting in complicated systems that couldn't do many things people find simple.[12] We generally don't think in rules, and translating heuristics and intuition to that form is limiting.

By the late 80s, when I was developing AI in graduate school, the approach began to change. Machine learning was born. Given examples of appropriate decisions—often human interpretations of data—computers could learn to emulate those decisions. My doctoral dissertation used machine learning to distinguish the electrical emanations of presumably healthy brains from those with Multiple Sclerosis (MS).[13]

Machine learning was a major paradigm shift in computer programming. Computers could be given instructions on how to learn to do something instead of being told exactly how to do it. If conventional computer programs are step-by-step recipes as in cooking, then machine learning is a program that learns how to create recipes.

I know this sounds like some sci-fi fantasy with the notion of machine learning giving you a popsicle headache. Can't computers only do what they are told to do by people? Sure...but the type of direction can come at many abstraction levels—as with instructing people.

Machine learning separates computer programming into two phases. In the training phase, a computer is given instructions on how to learn to process information rather than steps for processing it. Those learning instructions analyze examples of the task it is being trained to perform. Continuing the recipe analogy, it is presented examples of recipes that people made, and it follows computer code that learns the patterns of information in human-constructed recipes. The output of the learning phase is an AI model that can be very complex.

Once taught, the AI execution phase performs the pre-set calculations in the AI model on similar data not in its training examples. For example, an AI that learned about recipes might be used to generate a new recipe given a set of ingredients. We use AI in its execution phase, though some of the newest AI can do a small amount of learning in that phase (at the time it is used).

The how-to-learn instructions are abstract, math-laden steps, but the result is an algorithm that can do something after the training wheels are removed. AI machine learning is an algorithm (machine learning) that creates an algorithm (the AI model). AI models consist of tons of adjustable numbers (among other properties). The job of the learning software is to find the best set of those numbers (a.k.a. parameters) to do a certain task given the example data it is shown during training.

With machine learning, no longer did programmers have to tell computers exactly how to process information; now they could be programmed to learn to process.

The dawn of machine learning kicked off another wave of AI hype, but neither enough computing horsepower nor digitized training examples were available for most applications in my graduate school days.

AI did have practical applications in the 90s, but most were hidden from sight or of limited utility. It was often deployed to upgrade already automated systems like the control systems that monitor and run machines. Topics such as speech recognition became practical but for limited purposes.

In the 00s the advancement of computing power and data availability began to alleviate the bottlenecks that were holding back machine learning. The AI models could be bigger—important for more complex decisions—and the growth of data stores allowed training those bigger models.

A landmark paper in 2012 ushered in the next wave of progress. Researchers at the University of Toronto showed dramatic improvement in image recognition—a task easy for people but historically hard for machines.[14] It spawned a family of methods called "deep learning" that allowed the training of larger AI models using bigger data sets. Some of the math was decades old but became possible to use at bigger scale because there were faster computers and more data. Deep learning became a go-to approach for many applications. To use a hardware analogy, deep learning is a multi-purpose chip.

AI advancements started to go exponential. The type of exponential phenomena I'm referring to are those which grow (or shrink) as a multiple of itself. COVID-19 infection, by example, spreads more if there are more infected people (unless there are measures to prevent infection transmission). AI progress similarly builds on prior advancements. Deep learning and other "chips" became combined in creative ways, and the resulting multi-piece architectures were also shown to be reusable. Specialized AI hardware allowed training of much bigger AI models (training being the computationally intensive step).

AI abilities that rival or exceed human ones came with increasing frequency. AI could decimate previously automated chess algorithms (which already had beaten people), and even reign over Go, a much more complex game than chess that had escaped prior automation supremacy. AI could beat the best Jeopardy champions. It could interface to the Internet via voice-driven assistants...albeit with frustrating and sometimes laughable errors. It could translate language. It could interpret imagery in ways only people could previously accomplish, like in diagnosing abnormalities in medical images. Each advance was way faster than what many AI experts had expected.

By the 20s, some of the constraints on AI development and proliferation were crumbling. Various methods reduced the number of training examples needed to build it. Other ones allowed AI to teach itself by exploring the world (e.g., robotics) instead of relying on a pile of training data assembled by people. Techniques emerged to transfer what one AI learned to allow fast learning of another AI.

A couple of years ago I believed AI would be hugely impactful to every job—but not eliminate the knowledge-driven contributions of people for quite a while. Then came 2022. Now it seems inevitable that AI will exceed human abilities for a wide range of tasks. The AI community made a big bet that bigger AI models trained on bigger data sets would demonstrate emergent, more sophisticated behaviors. They were right.

CHATGPT

It came as a surprise to OpenAI employees. The company was formed to take a long-term view of AI capabilities. Its ethos was to focus on issues like safety and veracity over short-term profit. However, in November of 2022, right before Thanksgiving holiday week, staff got an unexpected task. Company leadership announced they wanted to release a chatbot (AI that can have conversations with humans)...in two weeks.

The company had already created a splash the year before with the release of its GPT-3 (Generative Pre-trained Transformer) language model. The underlying "transformer model" technology was widely understood although creatively adjusted by OpenAI engineers. Google researchers had published the transformer model technique in 2017[15], and all the big AI companies have been working on their own versions.

Transformer models are...well...transformative in large part because they learn so quickly. For decades one of the biggest obstacles for AI was it needed a lot of data to learn something. Transformers need tons of data too but can learn from data more efficiently. Training bigger AI models became computationally practical. Once trained, the model can learn new things with only a few more examples. In the case of GPT-3, many new language feats can be performed without having to go back to a lengthy and costly training process.

GPT-3 was a far bigger AI model than its predecessors. I mean really big. GPT-3 has 175 billion parameters—more than the roughly 120 billion neurons in the human brain. That model was about 1,000 times bigger than what came before it.[16]

OpenAI was betting that bigger AI would mean better AI. Not everyone in the AI community thought that would be the case. Yet

GPT-3 was clearly superior to known predecessors in both human qualitative observation and on numerical accuracy tests.[17] A bunch of companies began building products based on it. OpenAI didn't stop there. They began building the successor called GPT-4, which launched in March of 2023.

Some OpenAI workers were surprised about the chatbot release decision because it was a change in plan, and because inevitably there wouldn't be time to fully test the product that became called ChatGPT.

ChatGPT was based on an upgrade to GPT-3 which they termed GPT-3.5, but they had GPT-4 coming quite soon. Some employees— used to seeing the capabilities of GPT-4—thought "a chatbot built on a two-year-old A.I. model might seem boring."[18]

I should explain what ChatGPT can do, since calling it a chatbot connotes historically very limited customer service help on company web pages. ChatGPT was an eye opener. New uses continue to be discovered daily by creative users.[19] It can summarize complicated topics. It can give personalized recommendations. It can generate brainstorming ideas, translate text, converse in a specified style, offer suggestions for your writing, analyze the emotional tone of text, create test questions for teachers, and provide career or even mental health advice. Less well advertised is its ability to write computer code, new songs or poetry, or find data sets.

As an example, I asked it about the topic of Chapter 2—"What human qualities will AI not automate?"—and got the following answer:

"There are certain human qualities that are difficult to automate or replicate in artificial intelligence (AI). These include:

Creativity: AI can be trained to recognize patterns and generate new ideas based on those patterns, but it is difficult to replicate the creative process that humans use to generate original and innovative ideas.

Empathy: AI lacks the ability to truly understand and feel the emotions of others. While it is possible to program an AI to recognize and respond to certain emotions, it cannot experience empathy in the same way that humans do.

Social skills: AI lacks the ability to understand and navigate complex social situations and relationships in the same way that humans can. While it can be programmed to recognize and respond to certain social cues, it lacks the ability to truly understand and interpret the intentions and motivations of others.

Intuition: AI lacks the ability to make decisions based on gut feeling or intuition. It can only make decisions based on the data and information that it has been trained on.

Morality: AI lacks the ability to understand and adhere to moral principles in the same way that humans do. While it can be programmed to follow certain rules or regulations, it lacks the ability to truly understand and internalize the underlying moral reasoning behind these rules."

Perhaps you think it just plucked the text from some website since surely others have answered this question in some form. No...this text never existed before. The AI was trained on lots of information—some of which related to this question—but it answered the query on its own. From my vantage point it did a pretty good job.

ChatGPT wasn't the only 2022 splash for OpenAI. They also released DALL-E2, an upgraded version of their AI that creates images based on human language requests. It, and other products like it, caused quite a stir in artistic circles. Tell it to draw "A painting of a fox sitting in a field at sunrise in the style of Claude Monet" and it generates one of such quality that you could be forgiven for thinking it comes from a human artist.[20] This ability rides on GPT-3 to interpret the language prompt, and a second AI piece that treats the GPT-3 output as an image caption and finds pixels that correspond to such a description.

The hurry-up release of ChatGPT was based on nervousness, opportunism, or a combination of both. There were several other companies building their own language AI (large language models, to be precise). OpenAI leadership was afraid somebody would beat them to the market. They also figured they'd learn from the ChatGPT demo and apply those lessons to the GPT-4 product development and launch.

Yes...I did say demo. The company didn't expect it to become the sensation that it has. It took Instagram—previously the role model for fast growth—more than two years to hit a hundred million users.[21] It took ChatGPT two months to reach that threshold.[22]

THE IMPLICATIONS

ChatGPT has instigated crisis discussions in every school in the country and caused workers in many fields to wonder about their future. Lawmakers are talking about regulations. Some liken its capabilities to high-tech plagiarism.[23] Others worry about its accuracy or information traceability, or that propagandists can now turbo-charge misleading campaigns. The hype and concerns are so strong that OpenAI downplayed its own product[24] and lowered expectations for the GPT-4 release.[25]

Human-generated text (and images in the case of DALL-E2) was used to train the AI. That has rightfully brought many objections from artists and writers who get neither credit nor a piece of the rich AI proceeds. New models are needed to make sure people are not exploited.

ChatGPT and products like it are an inflection point in AI history. Absorbing that reality requires stepping back from the existing warts and doing only a small amount (a couple of years) of forecasting.

One of the near-term issues is that these products are frequently wrong—sometimes egregiously. The erroneous answers are concerning, but remember the appropriate comparison isn't to perfection, it's to what people can do, and people already "know" less than ChatGPT and are surely fallible. We already know that errors don't stop AI products from being used. If there's anything the past decade has taught us, it's that people and companies will take imperfect AI if it makes things much cheaper, or saves us time or energy. Those benefits can override an accuracy concern.

Besides, AI will get dramatically better very quickly. At the time of this writing, GPT-4 has just been released, and it is better performing across a variety of testing measures. For example, the original ChatGPT scored in the *lowest* 10% of legal bar exam takers. The new release that uses the upgraded GPT-4 scores in the *top* 10% on that exam.[26] That improvement happened in a few months.

I get it though. We have the tendency to believe what is presented authoritatively, and the nature of AI mistakes can be child-like, showing what it knows (a ton) and what it understands (nothing) are two different things.

The serious business uses are probably not as concerned with AI errors because they will continue to have people in the loop curating the AI output. That takes far fewer people than from-scratch creation (if producing the same amount of text). Plus, the human corrections can be used to retrain AI to improve its future answers. It's only a matter of time before less curation effort is needed. Remember too that most tasks are not life and death. There can be forgiveness for AI errors in many work situations.

Curation will be assisted by traceability of the AI answers. Microsoft—who owns a sizable chunk of OpenAI—has upgraded its Bing Internet search engine to include a ChatGPT variant. Many other products are similarly incorporating advanced chatbots. Bing provides web page links for the chat that make it easier to understand sources and accuracy. Other measures like uncertainty estimates should be doable extensions.

Another big complaint is that the AI can be misused. It could take propaganda to a whole new level, for example, with AI generating new content on its own, and without the propagandist needing to be a techie. It is a hugely important concern, and I have no idea what to do about it. I hope there are constructive discussions on the matter, but I fear that the knee-jerk will be in outlawing AI in various situations. That won't work. The horse has left the barn. Anyway, inserting appropriate AI controls is an important subject, but one beyond the scope of this book.

Educators are rightly freaking out about how this might impact the classroom. There need to be policies surrounding its use by students or teachers, but many of the measures will be band-aids. For example, there are numerous spinoff AIs that try to detect what text was Chat-GPT-penned. However, ChatGPT is only the beginning of a slew of such products...each with its own pros and cons. The AI models will continue to get better, and users will grow in sophistication. It will become harder to know if something was AI-generated unless you were involved in creating it.

Instead, workers and educators need to be looking further ahead. What does this mean in the broader context of human contributions, and what opportunities or challenges does such AI create?

First understand that this type of AI is different in a few important dimensions from what came before it. One long-held AI adage was that each instantiation could be used for one narrow purpose. Perhaps we can still say that in a technical sense. There is one objective for ChatGPT—to predict what should come next in text (an oversimplified explanation). However, that single technical objective results in a product that has myriad uses.

ChatGPT and products like it are building blocks for more customized AI. People can add their own data on top of it and have an AI model that can address a more specialized or personalized purpose. This blows way past single-use AI. It is a basis for other AI that can be built with little additional data because the underlying language model is so powerful. That's beyond AI "chips"—they're AI "boards." There's little stopping a company from having a variant that answers questions about the business or team activities within it. Nor should it be hard to tune it to be the expert for particular fields like medicine or law...or whatever yours might be.

It's not about ChatGPT *per se*. It's about the generality of these kinds of AI, their ease of use, and the small incremental effort that's needed to extend or customize its capabilities.

AI has hit public consciousness, but we've only begun to think about the implications. I am pretty sure next year will bring more AI surprises, as will the years that follow. This is only the beginning. Our minds must think forward to the broader implications. We need to move from tactics related to ChatGPT to a strategy that considers where AI is going and what that means for work, society, and education.

We make our livings largely because of expertise—the ability to have comprehensive and authoritative knowledge in a particular area. That's what our degrees are about. It's how we describe our professions. It's what we expect from the "what do you want to do when you grow up?" question.

The problem is that AI is gobbling expertise. It's now hard for me to see how AI will not be the dominant source of knowledge in every documented discipline...including artistic ones. Homo Sapiens will no longer be the most knowledgeable on the planet. AI will be the experts.

That's a weird thing to say given AI doesn't understand the meaning of its knowledge like a human expert would. ChatGPT is just providing a statistically likely pattern of words in response to a user's pattern of words. That doesn't feel like expertise, but it is by virtue of behavior rather than mechanism. Airplanes don't flap their wings like birds, but they still fly.

There's another, more silent, but hugely important AI progression—beyond expertise consumption. AI is democratizing. Soon the ability to build and customize AI can be under the control of any worker.

DEMOCRATIZATION

The mysterious and unconscious force of intuition was in overdrive one fall day in the late 10s. As it is wont to do, mine came in an "aha!" moment. It was sudden, integrated several life lessons, and has changed my world view.

I was in a large lecture hall at MIT Lincoln Laboratory—my thirty-year employer—listening to a seminar from Google. "Oh shit!" was my gut reaction. The lecturer was talking about AI developing other AI. I knew it was being explored but hadn't seen clear success. The speaker showed it was working!

Until then I believed the availability of developers would limit AI's reach. It takes a lot of skill to develop AI. Engineers need a daunting combination of software, math, and data science capabilities, and they must keep up with a field whose techniques and tools change constantly. When designing AI, the engineers must choose the method wisely and set up a learning architecture that has many fine-tuning options.

That high skill bar has resulted in a huge talent shortage. A 2017 estimate was that industry could use 10,000,000 AI developers, but the supply was 300,000—worldwide.[27] Colleges and mid-career training programs have produced many more since...but not enough. A bachelor's degree recipient with AI skill can earn a six-figure starting salary. For a Ph.D., that figure can be several hundred thousand dollars. Finding good AI workers is a combat sport.

The seminar told me the labor constraint wouldn't last. The AI developer shortage is temporary, or at least what we call AI development will be a very different job. The seminar speaker reported on research to get AI to design other AI, and it was working better than human engineering.[28] Mind blowing...but in retrospect not surprising. It is probably inevitable since all the ingredients are present. There are best practices in AI design. There are clear ways to measure AI performance (though they are insufficient). There are many built AI solutions. That means auto-AI algorithms have examples to learn from, including from examples it generates on its own. Note that AutoML AI handles aspects of making AI, not in deciding what AI to make. That remains a human skill for now.

Until that seminar, I thought future workers needed much more STEM training (Science, Technology, Engineering and Math) to be capable of developing and using AI and other modern technologies. On that day I realized that technical expertise is no different from other fields...it too can be automated. A certain amount of technical know-how—at least at a conceptual level—will always help. Understanding one's tools is important. It just won't be enough. If AI engineers can be replaced, then that's a bellwether for a broader change. Instead of coding and implementing AI methods, AI engineering will be more about choosing the right problem and training data, and creatively assembling AI "chips" and "boards." Technologists will do much more abstract and humanistic tasks than conventional STEM training supports.

Don't get me wrong. This AI-developing-AI thing isn't entirely ready for an average user. Some developers can use it—relieving them of the need to have advanced data science skill—but they still must know how to code...for now. AI is beginning to write software better than people, too.[29]

Reducing the need for AI engineers opens the long-tail markets that are defined by lots of small markets with different needs. The longest tail is when every user wants something different every time. AI's main thing is decision making, and every business, job, task, and worker is in a somewhat unique position...with different accompanying decisions. Decision making is a long-tail market. There will never be enough human developers to serve all those unique needs, but with AI as the developer, the long tail can be reached.

I'll be more concrete and describe a plausible path of one profession. I've chosen one of the most humanistic of jobs...one that you might think is relatively immune to AI—psychotherapy.

GLIMPSING THE FUTURE

Mona entered the field because she had been through tough times. She had made some bad decisions. It was a psychotherapist who had been there to help her crawl out every time. She considered hers a dear friend, though she knew it was destined to remain one-sided.

It wasn't a hard choice for Mona to become a therapist. It was the only part of her life that she was always sure of.

At first it was intimidating. New things always are. It didn't take long for her to realize the patients couldn't see her nervousness or uncertainty. They were in their own minds. She got confident quickly.

No patient was a textbook case. They often wanted some labeled condition that they could look up, but labels are simplifications of real people. People are lots of things. The officially blessed diagnoses are like sticks dropped haphazardly into a giant, disorganized pile. The outline of the bundle defines a scope through which the sticks explore, but most of the space is empty; the sticks take up a small fraction of the pile. Most of the bundle is air. Analogously, patients were usually in the empty space—somewhere between the official diagnoses. Mona was proudest of her ability to apply her expertise flexibly...to treat clients like individuals, not categories. She looked for patterns and indicators but found each person a unique puzzle.

Then everything started to change. Her halcyon early career became something entirely different. By the end of the transition, Mona wasn't sure what her job was anymore. She was still customizing for the individual but no longer had the connection with patients that she most enjoyed. All because of AI.

It started with patient monitoring outside the therapist's office. The fitness industry had lots of data on what people did, felt, and sometimes thought. That data reveals a lot. The way the phone jiggles when it is with you...which it inevitably is...gives away not just when you step, but all the fine details of how you're moving. The data hints at your activities and typical movements. Couple that with other information like heart rate, blood pressure, respiration, voice, and perhaps text, and AI could tell the difference between exercising and getting high. AI could detect depression, panic attacks, PTSD reactions, and sometimes psychotic episodes. It could assess whether a person is calm, stressed, ill, and probably how firm their poop is!

You may think few people would agree to such monitoring, but carrots and sticks both influenced AI acceptance.

Many patients felt they could benefit from seeing their time-evolving mental health pattern. It helped that data privacy concerns were met with increasingly sophisticated cyber protections, ensuring patient-controlled access to their own data.

The stick eventually came from the insurance companies. They had long wanted to go from a fee-for-service payment model to a fee-for-value paradigm. In other words, "we'll pay you (the health care provider) if you're doing it the right way." They wanted the right way to include health monitoring outside the therapist's increasingly e-office. The app homework became standard.

Psychiatrists were the first to see benefit from the collected information. Medication choices and adjustments were improved. Therapists later found value, too. They could see clear anomalies in the wearables data and compare them to patient reports.

With insurance company enforcement, a huge amount of data accumulated—if patients allowed such access—on therapy practices and the more continuous effect on patients. A lot more was learned about what was working, and it was AI that found those patterns. Mona started getting automated newsletters on the advancements in the field as more and more data was analyzed. The sheer volume of literature was oodles more than it had ever been, and it had always been beyond one brain.

Those data discoveries needed both the patient monitoring to assess impact, and the treatment strategies or visit summaries from the therapist, to tie cause to effects. The AI didn't stop at analyzing therapist notes. Patient records now included audio and sometimes video recordings of counseling sessions. It was initially resisted, but people got used to it. Medical records already had a ton of sensitive content anyway.

It turned out that therapy became cheaper, thus more widely accessible, when AI analyzed counseling conversations. It became a business advantage. At first AI used the voice and video information to estimate emotional and cognitive states during the therapy session, but that was just the beginning. The automation began to pull out the therapeutic approach from the session audio. AI assessed the patient's fit to several psychological conditions and states by the content of the conversations and subtle audio and facial features. Other AI could then pose comments to the therapist or suggest questions for the patient during the counseling session.

Mona didn't always like AI's dialog recommendations. Often the AI was choosing a question that best illuminated a diagnosis or treatment plan. Therapists frequently knew better. Information maximization wasn't always what the patient needed in that moment. Sometimes key information would take a while to tease out.

The AI's summary of a session was informative, though. At least it was an alternative view, and rarely did Mona think it was very far off-base. She learned from the automation's assessments far more than from digging through voluminous literature. AI gave her a short list of relevant research findings regarding each patient in case she needed it.

She had a bit of time to read up because the documentation workload was way down. Mona was reviewing documentation—not creating it from scratch. Usually she added a few more insights, but the AI summary was mostly right. It saved her a ton of time. AI-generated dashboards for each patient would suggest an approach for the next session and point out "what if" pivots for unforeseen issues the patient could bring up.

Eventually, Mona didn't need to be at counseling sessions at all. Therapy with a computer avatar was preferred by some patients. By the time AI had permeated all aspects of her practice, it could create an avatar that was hardly distinguishable from a real person.

For those who wanted a real flesh-and-blood therapist, the counseling roles could be filled with lower cost and less credentialed workers. They didn't need to understand much of psychology or even what to say during a session. AI took care of that. Their job was to read the person and occasionally override the AI when needed to establish a better connection with the patient. Mona called them Empathists.

The patient was better served by this increased scrutiny and attention to their health. More patients could be served because costs were lower and service availability was higher.

Mona felt the AI were now the experts. Before AI, many psychologists were not up to speed on the latest advances and treatment approaches. It's a lot of work to stay current. AI never got behind. Its massive knowledge networks were updated frequently with the latest and greatest.

Everything was different. Mona spends most of her time managing the AI and the Empathists. She knows she's still providing an important service, but oh how she misses the old days.

Mona is of course fictional, but the evolution of her job is consistent with AI's expertise-chewing march. Some of the capabilities—

such as mining the data from wearable devices—are works in progress (though little of it has gone through FDA oversight). [30]

The notion that counseling might use an AI therapist may seem to be the biggest stretch. Who would want to talk to a computer over a real person? It turns out virtual therapists are already in development, and some people (e.g., military personnel) prefer the computer one![31] The convenience of being able to talk to a virtual therapist at any time is also a competitive advantage over the human service. Plus, I suspect the trepidation over talking to a virtual therapist will decrease over time if the technology provides trustworthy guidance. It is reasonable to think Mona wouldn't want a fake therapist to resemble and behave too closely like her, but the ability for AIs to talk, look and behave in indistinguishable ways from real people is already a thing. They're called "deepfakes."

It isn't likely that psychotherapy would evolve in precisely this way. One can't discount technical obstacles, human acceptance, rollout slowness, and regulatory constraints, but the ingredients and methods are all pointing in the direction of Mona's fictional future job. My crystal ball will necessarily be off, but that future is plausible.

One thing is for sure—AI will change jobs. A lot. Nearly every job.

§

AI is as fundamental a change as electricity and computers, and it will certainly eliminate some jobs. Several efforts have been made to estimate the degree to which existing work tasks will be replaced by automation. Estimates go as high as half of current work disappearing.[32]

In comparison, I haven't seen estimates about how many jobs AI will create. Such a study would be hand-wavy at best. Prediction of current job evolution is hard enough, but at least it starts from a known basis—today's jobs. Prediction about tomorrow's jobs lacks any foundation.

Make no mistake though. AI will also create a lot of jobs and tasks.

Whether or not the Luddite fallacy has a breaking point is debatable, with some economists feeling there are fundamental constraints. For example, if AI could do everything better than people, who would buy it if everyone were out of work? Such an end point or anything close to it would require a major reworking of some of the fundamentals of society.

That isn't to say that everything will be chugging along as it has. Andrew McAfee at MIT and Eric Brynjolfsson at Stanford described the key issues and questions in their best-selling book *The Second Machine Age*. If AI can do a lot that people can do, they posit the problem will be "As digital labor becomes more pervasive, capable, and powerful, companies will be increasingly unwilling to pay people wages that they'll accept and that will allow them to maintain the standard of living to which they've been accustomed. When this happens, they remain unemployed."[4]

The concern is widening economic inequality. That's where economists tend to agree. They've been observing that trend for decades. Mean wealth and prosperity continue to increase, but that benefit is increasingly unequal. Haves and have-nots grow further apart.

One of the reasons McAfee and Brynjolfsson give for this is that digital technologies immediately have a global market, unlike physical work or many services. A better digital technology can quickly displace its competitors, creating winner-take-all situations that concentrate wealth. Another reason is that information technologies favor more skilled workers. That isn't to say that there are fewer overall jobs, but that those who cannot do the higher skill work are increasingly paid poorly.

The evolution of Mona's fictional psychotherapy practice shows how technology can cause this inequality. It's not the only cause, but it's a major one. Mona must be more skilled after AI insertion than beforehand. She still must know the psychology and have human interaction savvy, but she also needs to understand the technology she's using and anticipate paradigm shifts because of it. Chances are she is serving a bigger set of patients because automation can trim her costs and eliminate her time as the productivity bottleneck. That should mean she must understand a wider range of mental health conditions.

Mona's evolving practice created Empathist jobs. Though they might be numerous, they are lower skill positions than psychotherapy because AI handles the domain knowledge part of the job. The Empathists would be paid far worse than the therapists.

In the fictional scenario, nobody seems to be in the position psychotherapists once were. That job role was replaced with one at higher skill and many at lower skill, with the Empathist positions at risk of future automation from improved AI therapists. The same bifurcation is a reasonable future from a product like ChatGPT. That product will require high-skill people who can uncover the problems to be solved and creatively apply the AI, and lower-skill ones who do editing or fact checking.

Would the evolution change how many Monas are needed? Maybe not if there is a large market for therapy that can't be served by the conventional job model, and the automation helps decrease prices.

The key for education is to get as many workers as possible to the high skill side of the labor pool, where they can be one of the beneficiaries of AI and not a casualty of it. The data shows that the wage bump from extended education continues to grow.[33] Will there be fewer high-skill jobs than before? No...probably more. That has been the trend, plus higher-skill positions are increasingly ideation and innovation ones that stimulate the economy.

Unfortunately, the data also shows that beginning around 1980 (perhaps not coincidentally when personal computing emerged) education is no longer providing enough high-skill workers. In their book *The Race Between Education and Technology*, economists Claudia Goldin and Lawrence Katz from Harvard discuss the data and potential causes in detail.[34] They show that in recent decades we have not educated as many high-skill workers as needed, and that a lot of that can be explained by the inability to get the more disadvantaged to that skill level.

It's also possible that the educational model has become less relevant. This book claims it has. AI and other automations are stealing expertise roles in particular—the *raison d'etre* of conventional schooling. I argue that continuing that model will only lock-in the disturbing trend of concentrated wealth.

The concern I hear is that AI will take jobs. It will, and although new jobs will be created the disruption to individual lives could be significant. However, the long-term issue is that workers will need to be capable of the higher-skill work that is complementary to AI.

In Chapter 2, I describe the uniquely human roles that remain— those that leverage the skills of wisdom.

2.

HUMANITY'S WISDOM ROLE

The real problem is not whether machines think but whether men do.

B.F. Skinner[35]

Imagine you are given an out-of-the-blue question—one you have no expertise to answer. You'd likely use your favorite search engine and look for the answer...or maybe now your favorite chatbot...right?

What if the question is about the future? Should you still trust the search engine? Isn't prediction in the realm of opinion? In today's information-rich environment, knowing what to trust is at the heart of critical thinking. Should another expert's prediction be trusted, or does it have equivalent accuracy to tarot cards and crystal balls?

Let's say the question is about your business. What will the earnings be a year from now? What will the future market or competition look like? What changes will be needed in the people or machine aspects of the business, or in organization and culture? These are some of the questions every business should tackle, and there are similar questions regarding your profession or job that each employee should consider.

"Whew," you may think. That's in more of a comfort zone. You understand your business and its industry. You understand your profession, your job, and yourself. You can see the warts and the gems. When it comes to your business and your profession, you are the expert. Your forecast should be more accurate than some naïve person...right?

Professor Philip Tetlock at the University of Pennsylvania wondered if those who we regard as experts are better at forecasting. He posed this question in a geopolitical context in 1984. In the mid-80s, each political side in the U.S. was wondering what would happen to the Soviet Union. Would President Reagan's hard-line result in liberalization or retrenchment of the Soviets? Which of those directions would the new Soviet leader Mikhael Gorbachev take the country? If he chose reform—would he succeed? Both dove and hawk pundits had well-reasoned positions backed by their respective philosophies. Tetlock wondered how often such forecasts were right.

He started studying the egghead predictions.[36] Over decades, Tetlock ran several forecasting tournaments with thousands of players who made bets on the likelihood of geopolitical outcomes—with questions carefully posed to enable quantitative scoring.[37] The data he amassed has revealed far more than geopolitical forecasting prowess.

Players were challenged to forecast the outcomes of highly uncertain situations months to a year ahead of time. A logical first question is whether anyone would do well. He showed many experts were no better at prediction than a "dart-throwing chimpanzee," and some performed worse than random chance. Yet other players were consistently better than chance. Some were a lot better.[38]

One might expect that the best forecaster of the outcome of a Colombian election, for example, would be the expert in Colombian politics, or Colombia more generally, or maybe an election or political expert for another part of the world. In a statistical sense that's not the case. The best forecasters in Professor Tetlock's tournaments weren't the domain experts. They tended to be people who had domain-transcendent skills.[39]

Extrapolating to business strategic planning, this result suggests that the best strategic forecaster may not be you or others in your company. Complete outsiders might do better.

Tetlock isn't saying just anyone will do better. He noted that strong forecasting requires people with certain qualities and mental approaches in addition to broad perspectives. He called them super-forecasters.

The world is increasingly calling for forecasts that involve more uncertainty. The dramatic pace of change means the world of tomorrow may be little like the world of the past...devaluing extrapolations. Anyone involved in strategic planning knows it is a highly inexact endeavor—one often dominated by personalities and wishes more than information and realism.

Tetlock says the best forecasters are foxes, not hedgehogs. The analogy is based on a quote from the Ancient Greek poet Archilochus. He wrote "the fox knows many things; the hedgehog, one big thing." Philosopher Isaiah Berlin used Archilochus' analogy in a 1953 essay that divided thinkers into hedgehogs—who view the world through the lens of one idea, and foxes—whose varied experiences don't allow a unifying simplification. [40]

Hedgehogs are the domain experts in this analogy. Hedgehogs have a deep, relevant knowledge base, and that's a big advantage. There are disadvantages too. Experts can become too confident in their knowledge or theories. They may have a subconscious tug toward the status quo that has given them status. Tetlock's data shows this tendency; the deep experts make forecasts with more certainty, and they're less likely to revise their forecasts when new information is available.[41] They may be so immersed in the thinking of their domain, and have experiences largely within that realm, that it forms its own echo chamber—as we have seen with political affiliations.

The foxes (a.k.a. jack-of-all-trades) are the superforecaster analogs. They will focus more on the context, the analysis process, a more complete range of possibilities, how prior forecasts went right or wrong, and explicit identification of doubts. They're more comfortable with uncertainty and less certain of themselves. They're ready to change their minds if information points that way. They aren't as interested in showing decisiveness as the deep experts. Prudence, or being wrong, does not impose the same ego hit.

That relative humility also makes them strong teammates—at least with other foxes. When the superforecasters were assembled into a prediction team, the entire team did better than each of the individual superforecasters, and better than expert groups.[38] It wasn't a fluke. The margin between the superforecaster team and its competition grew over time. They were better together. Some likely expected the super-group would have ego battles instead.

The fox forecast strategies are teachable. Other forecasters were taught to use superforecaster strategies. With just an hour of prior instruction, other forecasters would perform statistically better—even a year later.[38]

That some people did much better than others at predicting highly uncertain future events may seem irrelevant to business, or personal, or to any other kind of forecasting. That caution is warranted to some degree. The expert part of me—the scientist—knows that the validity of Professor Tetlock's results are not proven more generally. If a superforecaster were put into a situation that requires predicting individual human behavior and emotions, for example, that skill might not correlate with forecasting a geopolitical situation.

Yet the intuitive part of me says there is more here—much more. The foxes had certain characteristics: wariness of kneejerk answers, a focus on analysis and decision processes, broad knowledge, and intellectual humility. Those are not likely to disappear when faced with a forecast of another type.

All nontrivial work tasks require forecasting the outcome of the work and how useful it might be. It's how people or their bosses decide what work to prioritize, what approach to take to the work, and what to do with productive output. Decision making inherently includes a prediction element. Our brains predict all the time. We can't function in the world without that ability. Prediction is at the heart of other skills like critical thinking or social interaction. It isn't some weird professorial topic; it's critical to everything we do.

The brain's cognition isn't a one-way road from sensing to action. We also incorporate feedback and planning. Our barrage of perceptions converts to more abstract interpretations before an action or a behavior results. Conscious intent, prior experience, and emotional states all factor into decisions.

It is quite easy to show that forecasting is a necessary precursor to action. The delay in processing information—especially for our relatively slow neurons—means even routine actions like body movement must be a bit predictive. Prediction of how the world might evolve or react to your actions is also key to forming a model of how the world works. Professor Tetlock's results seem generally relevant to how people decide.

Forecasting isn't the only realm that demonstrates non-expert forte. The value of outsider perspectives in innovation is well established.

In the first chapter I described how AI is changing the nature of labor. Workers are being pushed toward a narrower value definition... one less defined by expertise. The work remaining for people uses more superforecaster skills—those conventionally associated with wisdom.

THE EROSION OF HUMAN CONTRIBUTIONS

It is one of the oddities of aging that at some point we sound like melancholy tourists in the modern world. The comparisons to "when I first started" trickle from our mouths. Outside of our contemporaries, we just sound out of touch or worse yet like we're pining for the good ol' days. I think it's as much a reflection of our intermittent surprise as it is nostalgia. Work is so different now. So is life. Change has been dramatic—dizzyingly fast compared to long-term history, and to the pace our brains and institutions were built to handle.

My first professional job was as a summer intern in the mid-80s for a large manufacturing company. They were also pioneers in computer technology.

I worked in a business unit responsible for negotiating the supply chain for their products. Most of the workers had at least a few gray hairs…if they had much hair at all. Women were scarce except in administrative roles. It was typical for a worker to have been in some form of the same job for many years.

My presence was part of a big evolution for those workers. It was the beginning of the personal computer era. Oh sure…there were other changes. There was a product quality push, the beginning of just-in-time inventories, and increasingly international suppliers. Smoking in the office would end in the years that followed but not for that summer. I smelled like a smoker each day without ever touching the stuff.

Computers were different than those other reforms—they immediately made experts into novices. Men had never been trained to type. These days we take typing for granted, as children and keyboards are inseparable, but in the 80s it was a distinguishing skill. Men who were lucky to have able typists could delegate all computer work to their staff. That continued for a long time. I am aware of executives in the late 90s who had their secretaries (as they were then called) print out their emails so they could edit them manually, after which the secretary typed the response.

The coopting of mental skills was more impactful than typing deficiency. The buyers' job at this company required not only the interpersonal skills of negotiation, but also understanding of the details of the part they were acquiring, currency conversion rates, the historical reliability and quality of that supplier, and numerous other details. The best workers had most of that in their heads. Those memories were a big part of their work value.

I was there to help upend that. I worked on software that created an interface for the buyers into a database containing supplier and part information. The buyers didn't have to remember anymore—computers remembered. That the computer experts were inevitably young like me added to the insult. It's a tech-driven characteristic that has been remarkably sticky to this day.

Those buyers were terrified of computers and not only because of typing and the unreliability of that era's hardware. The change to their sense of stability and worth was dramatic. It meant a less skilled person could now do their job.

That change in worth drove the original Luddites. The textile machines weren't new. The artisans who broke machines were skilled at using them. They didn't especially hate technology.[42] They hated poverty and some business owners. Britain's economy was struggling after the Napoleonic wars. Unemployment and hunger were common, and it hit the artisan class hard. Their skills had given them immunity to prior downturns, but businesses dealt differently with the early 1800s situation. They began hiring cheaper...and the Luddites felt...more inept workers. Craftsmen were losing their jobs, and they felt textile quality was suffering. Taking out the machines was a protest against lower-skill labor—not the machines *per se*.

One could argue that technology is the single biggest long-term societal engineer. It's rivaled by crises like war, disease, and famine, but technology usually induces a permanent change. Impactful technology changes the way we work, live, or think. It drives cultural and societal change. Would the civil rights movement have made such rapid strides in the 60s without television? Would women have had the power and liberty to enter the workforce without the birth control pill? Would gay rights have advanced as much if treatments hadn't made HIV/AIDS a chronic condition versus a lethal disease?

I'm talking about technology in the broad sense, including fire, the wheel, and the invention of agriculture, which were all the rage back in the day. Cooking our food, for example, allowed us to fuel ourselves in less time (cooked food is more easily digested) and with less risk of disease. Farming meant that humans could stay in one place, and populations could increase. Specialist jobs sprouted as farming became more efficient so not everyone had to deal with food collection or preparation. Animals were enlisted not just as food sources but as labor sources. (Unfortunately, farming also meant children became part of the labor force, unlike with hunter-gatherer societies.)

Some job mechanization had incrementally sprouted by the beginning of the Industrial Revolution, but when mass production fully took hold, it changed the nature of work. In the 1840s nearly 70% of Americans were involved in farming. In 2000 that percentage was 2%.[43] Relatively few Americans now make a living off their physical strength. Sure...lots of jobs are physical; but for many of those positions the craftsmanship, improvisational skills, and fine motor skills reign supreme, not physical muscle power. Much of the effort is in controlling machines.

The service industry blossomed as production jobs decreased. Machines could replace muscles but not brains. Throughout the 20th-century, the most skilled service positions relied on lots of remembered knowledge and the management of specialized labor. Schooling became mandatory as workers otherwise would not have the right skills. Specialization was amplified. By the time computers were introduced to the workplace, many careers were based on deep understanding of specific knowledge domains. College degrees were defined by those knowledge sectors...and still are.

Computers and predecessors like calculators consumed repetitive math tasks that were a big part of scientific jobs. The science world in transition to computers was shown well in the movie *Hidden Figures*, which was about woman pioneers at NASA in the moon-launch era. Detail-oriented labor...before computers and automated instruments...was more prevalent than just at NASA, or for math. Chemists were running experiments by hand. Accountants kept manual books. The work was repetitive but required high accuracy. Many were employed as administrators of knowledge.

General-purpose computers allowed more complex calculations, but its more pervasive influence is in acquiring, organizing, and disseminating information. Most professions had to handle increasingly voluminous information. Written information slowly ceded to computerized versions (in some fields that march continues). A wide swath of administrative and process jobs quietly disappeared since computers could do it more efficiently. New jobs were created to manage the computers.

Machines eat away at the contributions that we can make to work. Some of our brain power—the ability to remember stuff—doesn't have the currency it once did. Knowledge is still important, but figuring out what information is needed and what is extraneous are more important than memorizing.

Jobs have tilted toward selecting and interpreting information rather than acquiring and remembering it. Tasks have migrated from mindlessly repetitive to less trivial decision making. Work effort still matters, but it matters less than it once did. Making good judgments and congealing work with a team supersedes elbow grease. Effort in the wrong direction is unproductive, and with computers replacing a lot of human effort, the skill in choosing the most beneficial work path takes priority.

The computer era, along with other social changes, induced a pace of change that affected the notion of a job for life. By the end of the 20th century, it was common for people to change jobs. Now it's becoming common for people to go through a few different careers—not only different jobs.

Many jobs went away or changed their nature. Other tasks took their place, and new fields were created. Some of the remaining work became lower skill, as human memory was coopted by computer memory. However, the new fields tended to be higher-skill ones that are heavily reliant on characteristics like collaboration, judgment, reason, decision making, and sense making (the art of interpreting information). Jobs increasingly span disciplinary silos. Fox qualities are of growing usefulness, while hedgehog ones have become less important.

Then comes AI. More cherished human skills are whittling away to increasingly smart machines.

The new work climate demands we be adaptable to new challenges, including ones that formal education did not prepare us for. We can't afford to be tech avoidant like many during the PC revolution. Computerization required a massive change in infrastructure.

Moore's law (the doubling of computing power every couple of years) took some time.

In contrast, AI proliferates quickly since it rides on top of computing, wireless connectivity, and the Internet. Each new AI has a minimal incremental distribution cost. With the automation of coding and AI engineering, the creation cost is low too. AI can go from idea to realization in days or weeks. The pace of change is getting another turbo-charge.

We're running out of time to develop many more wise foxes. AI and other technologies are moving faster than our ability to retrain. Only in recent years has software development begun to gain traction in K-12 schooling, and yet AI will soon do much of the coding. Our retraining pace is far slower than the pace of technical advancement—a key distinction from earlier technology waves.

Decades ago...while AI was a vague, someday possibility...many in the education world noticed that major changes were needed.

21ST-CENTURY SKILLS

Every major education system in the world has emphasized the acquisition of detailed knowledge with more focused specialization as schooling progresses. Gaining expertise requires knowing a lot of detail. Schools are expertise factories. Education creates hedgehogs.

The education world hasn't been ignoring the trends. There is broad consensus on the need for so-called 21st-Century Skills that emphasize wisdom-related qualities.

It started from various directions, most ignominiously from a report called *A Nation at Risk* in 1983 that changed the course of American education, or...cynically...locked it in place.[44] A committee of eighteen members produced it based on the view of Reagan's Secretary of Education that the widespread experimentation with curriculum and teaching methods in the 60s and 70s was damaging, and that U.S education was failing in comparison to international systems.

From my own point of view, especially in elementary school (1967-73), the approaches were inconsistent. My second-grade math class was entirely self-paced. The teacher sat at her desk at the front of the room with folders of prescribed lessons and their progression. Students would take the next lesson and work it entirely on their own. The teacher was ostensibly there to help, but there were social disincentives in asking for it. Hyperactive and testosterone-charged boys like me turned it into a competition for speed and lesson level. Those who weren't getting it as easily watched a constant parade of other kids to the front of the room to grab the next lesson. Their academic performance was on public display. By the end of second grade, I was doing sixth-grade math; but third through sixth grade was conventional teaching that didn't allow racing ahead. My resulting boredom got me in a lot of trouble.

Meanwhile, the second-grade nun who taught reading and writing was all about memorization and neat penmanship. She had a strong punishment system. Her favorites were making us sit on our hands or kneel for long periods. I was on the kneeler a lot. Later, when self-paced grammar instruction emerged, in I think 4th or 5th grade, I was the one struggling more than others.

For a policy report, *A Nation at Risk* had inflammatory language. The most notable got newscast prominence—"If an unfriendly foreign power had attempted to impose on America the mediocre educational performance that exists today, we might well have viewed it as an act of war." It played on the national security concerns of the day, and echoes of that refrain continue. Some of the committee members stated afterward that they were not examining the assumption of U.S. education failure, but rather taking it as fact and devising remedies.[45]

The thing is the motivations were wrong. Educational achievement wasn't decreasing. Falling SAT scores from the early 60s through the 70s was central to the motivation for committee formation; except when Sandia Laboratories examined the data in 1990, they found differently.[46] The average scores did decrease over that time, but the reason was a different test population from the beginning to the end of that period. In the early 60s, mainly top students took the SAT, but by the 80s a much bigger percentage of the population was going to college, including more mediocre students. It wasn't failure. It reflected more in the population having college opportunity. The Sandia analysis struggled to get the same airtime and was actively censored.[45]

A Nation at Risk is liberal in its recommendations, essentially recommending more of everything: math, English, science, social studies, art, and more time in school. Among their recommendations was standardized tests, especially for transition from high school to college. The testing emphasis has only deepened in the 21st century. Standardized test requirements were strengthened in this century with the *No Child Left Behind* [47] legislation and the *Every Student Succeeds Act*.[48]

The U.S. Department of Labor took a different perspective, focusing on the workplace skills of the future. The Secretary's Commission on Achieving Necessary Skills (SCANS) reported in 1991, through interviews with business owners, managers, workers, and union officials, that more than knowledge competency was now required for workplaces.[49] The skills they prioritized weren't math, language, science, and social studies. They were abilities regarding resources, information, systems, technology, and interpersonal skills. Those recommendations rode on top of foundations in traditional school subjects, but the inclusion of thinking skills and personal qualities was a significant turn.

Other policy efforts were converging on similar views, though the language varied. Perhaps the most influential was generated by the now-coined Partnership for 21st Century Learning, or P21, founded in 2002 as a government-industry non-profit collaboration. Among their lexical contributions has been the Four C's of 21st-century learning: collaboration, communication, critical thinking, and creativity.[50] The Common Core Standards, issued in 2010, had a slightly different list.[51] There are several other recommendation lists with similar language that are collectively lumped under 21st-Century Skills. While differently labeled, they each ask for the improvement of humanistic, big-picture, and adaptive qualities. In my shorthand, they ask for wisdom—not expertise.

The demand signal from the business community has been consistent with the 21st-Century Skill philosophy...across many analyses now spanning multiple decades.[52] Business is asking for adaptable, creative people who show excellent judgment skills, communicate well, and are strong teammates. Much farther down the wish list is domain knowledge. They are also saying they can't find enough people with those skills.

Despite the desires of 21st-Century Skills, which most educators I have met have little quarrel with, schools are not focused on those skills. Knowledge stuffing still reigns supreme in most classrooms. Progress is impeded by the oil-and-water nature of expertise and wisdom learning environments (more on that later), and by the momentum and sometimes the retrenchment of mindsets.

The messaging of 21st-Century Skills has also been muddled. That hit home when I was at an education technology conference shortly before the pandemic struck. After a day of listening to speakers tout different needs such as critical thinking and interpersonal skills, a teacher got to the crux. He asked, "How am I supposed to make progress against such a long list of priorities?" There were a lot of nodding heads in the crowd. There is still confusion—decades after the 21st-Century Skills were defined. It seems to be a laundry list instead of a unified theme.

COMPLEMENTING AI

It has been demonstrated across a wide range of tasks that the combination of people and AI can be better than either is individually. People and AI have different strengths and weaknesses. Therein lies our salvation. That remains true with the latest AI advances, although the boundary is shifting.

I haven't really given you a clear description of what AI can do and people cannot. I'm saying AI will serve expertise roles and humans the wisdom functions without having defined those nebulous terms clearly. I will in the next section. For now, I'll attempt a unifying way to look at AI abilities. In doing so I am oversimplifying by choosing one facet or one family of AI over another. It's a bit like trying to summarize another person.

Many have attempted to characterize the tasks AI will consume. Often AI is couched as doing routine tasks...ones that are commonly performed. This derives from the idea that AI needs a lot of examples in its training process, either from humans doing the task or because the AI can generate its own examples by interacting with the world. Those examples are voluminous only if the accompanying task is common. AI that is intended to detect possible breast cancer from mammogram images needs lots of examples of the decisions that doctors made when analyzing those images. AI would handle typical images, while people would be responsible for the novel situations (borderline cases the AI didn't get enough examples of), or for the other aspects of diagnosing breast cancer...beyond imaging. The AI would on average be less capable if the task is less routine, if key information for the task isn't digitized, or if the examples it learns from are unrepresentative of past or future task situations.

The routine versus non-routine division of labor is less applicable for more recent AI, or I should say that it's still true, but the nature of the tasks AI is tackling are more abstractly defined. ChatGPT's fundamental task is transforming one set of characters (a user query) into another set (its generated text). That task is so general that it fits many different use contexts that appear nonroutine from the human point of view. Additionally, new forms of AI learning that can be done without tons of data examples have emerged. The routine versus non-routine distinction between human and AI task abilities is dissolving.

I think another way to couch AI ability—understanding there are many different methods under the AI umbrella that could each be spun differently—is puzzle solving. Puzzles in a very general sense have an explicit goal and a defined set of parts (perhaps abstract ones) that can be used for accomplishing that goal. In the breast cancer example, the parts are the image pixels, and the goal is agreement with what human experts would decide. In the ChatGPT example, the parts are characters, and the goal is generating text that has the best statistical agreement with what the people who created the training data text might have said. The puzzle characterization is also imperfect, but it captures better the important axes which are becoming less about how routine a task is and more about the nature of the problem and potential solutions.

Figure 1 illustrates the portion of problem and solution space that AI and humans contribute to. The two columns divide the challenge type: closed-ended, where the desired outcome is known, and open-ended, where best is debatable. The rows regard what tools or information can be brought to the solution. If there are defined ways to do something, that's closed-means. If new approaches are ok, that's open-means. The columns relate to the squishiness of the goal, and the rows are about solution constraints.

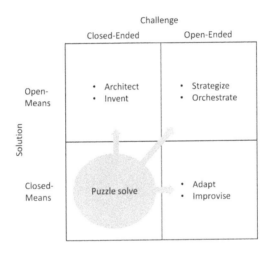

Figure 1. Pressures on human cognition from AI. The AI capabilities are in the lower left quadrant, with influence on human work in the other quadrants.

AI's puzzle solving lives in the lower-left quadrant. It is demonstrating convergent creativity...the ability to put together pieces in a unique way. Think of it as within-the-box creativity. I am not saying AI is creative in the way we think of that term. Chess-playing AI isn't devising a new strategy explicitly like people might in showing convergent creativity. It's just analyzing information patterns linking potential moves to eventual game outcomes. Nevertheless, its output can look creative. The easier it is to measure success, and the more obvious the puzzle pieces, the more likely AI will be doing it.

Fortunately for humanity, real-world problems are rarely closed-ended and closed-means. We usually have liberty to devise new approaches or solution pieces, and our challenges are often hard to define and have qualitative, multi-objective aspects so that "best" is a matter of values and priorities that humans will control. Those challenges involve divergent creativity—out-of-the-box thinking—that AI can't handle.

The art of using AI at work is figuring out the nature of the puzzle it should be given. As new capabilities like ChatGPT show, these puzzles are increasingly abstract. We creative humans will figure out how to define tasks in ways that AI can help...essentially broadening the size of the puzzle-solving quadrant. Humanity can still be in charge, but being in charge means having those wisdom-oriented, intangible 21st-Century Skills.

EXPERTISE VERSUS WISDOM

Merriam Webster defines an expert as "one with the special skill or knowledge representing mastery of a particular subject."

Definitions of wisdom are more varied, usually using words like judgment, discernment, experience, prudence, or sensibility. Those who research wisdom aren't in agreement on its meaning.

I am framing expertise and wisdom as distinct and complementary aspects of intellect that differ in at least the following dimensions:

- Detail-oriented (expertise) versus wholistic (wisdom);
- Perspective dominated by one knowledge domain (expertise) versus perspectives from many disciplines (wisdom);
- A focus on knowledge or tools (expertise) versus challenges (wisdom);
- Less (expertise) versus more (wisdom) problem complexity, abstractness, and uncertainty.

It isn't fair for me to couch expertise and wisdom as entirely distinct. Sparklingly clear boundaries are not comfortable companions with the vagaries of abstract language. Each of the comparative dimensions in the preceding bullets are sliding scales.

I do so for a couple of reasons.

One is that the school transformation I am advocating in this book is monumental. It must be a movement, and movements need clear messaging that people can implicitly understand, including a sharp contrast between then and now. Despite the vague definitions, I think the connotations of the words are consistent between people. I tried on other monikers, but they weren't as strong a fit.

The way I've distinguished expertise and wisdom also maps to aspects of our brains and the different ways they learn. I'll discuss that much more in the coming chapters.

Here I must make an impassioned plea. Do not mistake my emphasis on wisdom skills as a diminishment of expertise or those who display it. I am not against expertise. It's at least as important as wisdom. They are the Yin and Yang of thinking—contrary in many ways, but highly interdependent. Expertise has been responsible for enormous progress in the health and wellbeing of most people on the planet.

The problem is the emphasis between the two is off relative to their value in the AI age. That imbalance is visible across society. We laud game show contestants, chess grand masters, and spelling bee champions. Subjects requiring the most training to master piles of details—like for law, medicine, and other sciences—are used as mind measures as much as credentials. The historical esteem for sagacity seems to have eroded as provability and precision gained prominence.

It is funny to me that I was awarded a Doctorate of Philosophy (Ph.D.). The word "philosophy" derives from the Greek "philosophia," or "love of wisdom." However, every Ph.D. program I've seen requires multiple years of study in a very narrow realm—sometimes ones that are shared by few others on the planet. It's hardly possible to demonstrate multiple perspectives, for example, if a Ph.D. student is encouraged to dig deeper, not look more broadly. A Ph.D. is an oxymoron—more about expertise than wisdom. It's just one of the hidden prejudices of an expertise-dominated culture.

Wisdom involves making effective judgments using many perspectives and ideas, applying knowledge and experience in sound and fruitful ways, being mindful of complexities and nuances, understanding more so than knowing, and the ability to consider different ideas and perspectives. There is little provability and precision in any of that. Nevertheless, some are better at it than others. I hope they're also better at it than machines.

§

I led AI research and development for much of my career. A critical part of that work was making sure the AI addressed the right challenge. We needed help from workers or industry leaders who understood the domain better than us scientists. They'd inform why things are done the way they are and how the work paradigms might change with a technology insertion. After all, the most impactful technologies change operations in substantial ways.

Unfortunately, domain experts were often weak at thinking about such change.

I once spent a day with a major city police department discussing how automation might help investigations involving video data. I spent a couple of hours with an officer whose full-time job was analyzing video. Her routine task was to rapidly find video related to 911 calls. If she could look at the video and describe the scene to patrol officers before they arrived, then they might be in a better position to handle the situation appropriately. They weren't using any automation to process their video—just eyeballs and the fast forward button.

In between the 911 calls, she helped detectives with criminal investigations. The night before I arrived there had been a shooting where cameras were abundant. Eyewitnesses reported the vehicle type (e.g., red SUV) that was potentially involved. I watched her manually pull up camera footage and fast forward through the relevant period looking for that vehicle type. The entire path of the vehicle was desired which could require analyzing footage from hundreds of cameras. The task would take hours, and watching this video for more than a few minutes would put anyone into a virtual coma.

I was patient for a while because I didn't want to bias what technology enhancements she would want, but eventually I had to ask. "Would you like to enter a vehicle description and time period into a video search engine and be shown clips of all of the red SUVs and where they were in the road network?" Her face lit up. "You can do that?!" She had a hard time imagining her job being very different.

I had similar conversations with many users. The vision myopia isn't limited to police. It existed in every user community I dealt with, but especially in safety-related domains such as aviation safety, public health, disaster management, homeland security, and some corners of the military. Their mindset was inherently cautious, to avoid screwing up the whole system. They were tepid with changing operational paradigms. The answers to "what do you want?" were often surprisingly dull even when allowed a science-fiction wish list. Scientists and innovators could also be unimaginative regarding operational problems and constraints. Mental biases and roadblocks affect everyone.

A select few—I call them super-users—often supplied most of the insight. Somehow, they were less stuck in the mental traps of habits, norms, and paradigms. Super-users are like superforecasters, and both seem rare. The superforecaster label was applied to only two percent of Tetlock's already cognitively talented participants.

I am not pretending that forecasting equals wisdom, but it is a key characteristic which if poorly formed might preclude wisdom. Prediction is core to brain function. The neuroscientist Dean Buonomano describes prediction's role in memory. "Memory did not evolve to allow us to reminisce about the past. The sole evolutionary function of memory is to allow animals to predict what will happen, when it will happen, and how best to respond when it does happen."[53]

There are other ingredients to wisdom...beyond prediction skill...but we have few data sets like Professor Tetlock's. Unusual too might be great leaders, or the insatiably curious, or those who can be comfortable in the uncertain—if only we could rate such qualities consistently and accurately.

Wisdom researchers debate how to measure it, but none of the wisdom measures they've devised has been applied to many people. The most common measurement approach is to put people in specific, complex, and nuanced situations and have them speak on different perspectives and solutions regarding the problem.[54] That will sound familiar when I write later about gaming as a learning tool. Wisdom and its constituent talents aren't obvious from knowledge or even some conceptual queries; it is evident in addressing complex questions in specific contexts that require nuanced answers.

The work world has been asking for more wisdom skill for at least a few decades. Education hasn't been delivering enough wisdom for the workplace despite the 21st-Century Skill intentions.

People complement AI when we have information it does not, and that information is used to make more effective decisions. The undigitized situational context, and our understanding of how knowledge and concepts fit together, is our information edge. The question is whether people leverage that big-picture advantage. Tetlock's forecasting data and my user-interaction experiences suggest not many people are good at it. The superforecasters and super-users are unusual. The rest add little value over coin tosses. If we can't be better at skills like forecasting judgment, then the wisdom work might be automated too—regardless of AI's information and understanding deficit. AI can make coin flips too.

Consider CICERO...a relatively unheralded but significant AI demonstration from Meta AI in 2022. CICERO was taught to play the game Diplomacy. I won't go into the details of the game, but it is fundamentally about understanding and manipulating players to achieve a certain goal. According to Meta AI,

"Diplomacy has been viewed for decades as a near-impossible grand challenge in AI because it requires players to master the art of understanding other people's motivations and perspectives; make complex plans and adjust strategies; and then use natural language to reach agreements with other people, convince them to form partnerships and alliances, and more. CICERO is so effective at using natural language to negotiate with people in Diplomacy that they often favored working with CICERO over other human participants." [55]

CICERO ranked in the top ten percent of players who played multiple games. The other players weren't aware that CICERO was non-human. In a game where success requires building trust, AI did superbly.

On second thought, let me amend my earlier point. People will have to do *much* better than coin flips on wisdom-related skills.

The wisdom skills espoused by the 21st-Century Skill philosophies can't be add-ons in schools. They need to be the central objectives, or we risk competing with AI instead of collaborating with it. We will lose that contest.

However, AI can't be the only driver of a wisdom pivot. Highly impactful AI is relatively new, and the need for wisdom skills in the workplace emerged decades ago. Something more fundamental is driving the need. I think it's increasing complexity—the subject of the next chapter.

3.

WICKED COMPLEXITY

Some problems are so complex that you have to be highly intelligent and well informed just to be undecided about them.

Laurance J. Peter[56]

By the third week of January 2020, I was yelling at the TV. "What are you waiting for?" I shouted. I think my kids thought it weird. I can be animated, but not typically at the TV.

I wanted a travel ban from China. I knew it wasn't a panacea; there were a lot of reasons travel screening might not work, and we didn't yet understand the virus. I considered it a sign that we were taking it seriously. It was a week or two later when the U.S. Government enacted a highly leaky travel ban with China.

I had an early gut feeling that we were in deep doo-doo. I spent a decade at MIT Lincoln Laboratory leading research to combat biological weapons and natural pandemics. That stint included plenty of analyses for the U.S. Government on what could happen and what to do about it. We addressed questions about the damages that could result from various pathogens and infection routes, how to detect events quickly, what interventions would mitigate the impacts, and what could go wrong along the way. We analyzed a variety of situations, since a robust defense requires adaptability. I had seen and played with models of prospective situations enough to arm myself with intuition about large-scale infectious disease outbreaks.

A lot of that intuition was about what kinds of pathogens and infection routes can cause a rapidly growing outbreak. I figured COVID-19 had to be airborne well before there was evidence to support that. Historical viruses don't spread that quickly via fomite transfer (touching a contaminated surface). The wiping of surfaces maybe gave people a sense of control, but it couldn't be the main source of spread. Body fluid exchange routes, like sexual contact or blood transfer, tend to affect health-care settings and other specific demographics.

It had to have hit the Chinese quickly. We went from silence about it to Wuhan having thousands of infected. Even in an authoritarian state interested in keeping it quiet, hiding an outbreak that large would eventually fail. Nor was it likely that China would ignore it. By mid-January we knew the virus that causes COVID-19 was similar to SARS-CoV-1. That virus caused an outbreak in the early 00s in China and elsewhere that the world barely kept from mushrooming. China knew SARS-related viruses are serious business.

Since it was a new virus, the population likely wouldn't have immunity, meaning the infection would grow exponentially unless something major was done. In exponential processes, there can be an extended period where it appears not much is happening. The disease can stay below the radar until suddenly it is too big to handle. Even while wishing for travel restrictions, I knew there was probably plenty of time for the virus to have escaped Wuhan.

Exponential growth is a decision maker's bane. Actions must be taken before things have gotten out of control...while it doesn't look so bad. Those who had a gut understanding of the iceberg below the surface...and that our disease surveillance capabilities wouldn't likely pick up the illness until it was prevalent in a community...were sounding early alarm bells. The alarm was ringing in my head. I had experience thinking about bad disease outbreaks.

Yet my biggest takeaway from the pandemic is how little I had thought through the societal impact of such an outbreak and the difficult tradeoffs in managing it. Consideration of the economic, psychological, behavioral, and political aspects weren't a big part of my experience. One of the underlying assumptions I had was that people would behave in ways that protect themselves and their families from the infection. I discounted the other parts of the whole-world, complex system that the virus disrupted.

My naivetes were shared by many others. It's safe to say that no one person had a complete handle on COVID-19, its impacts, and what to do about those. Systems that were designed to work within certain limits were suddenly pushed beyond them. Whole industries ground to a halt. Supply chains fell apart. Relationships were breached. Shadow fears came into the light. The world system was moved to a new state, and the system is one of such enormous complexity that no person could make sense of it all.

The complexity wasn't solely because of the scale of the situation. There was uncertainty about the state of many pieces of the system and of their reaction to interventions. That went beyond uncertainty about the virus. Human behavior also drove the system, and human behavior always carries uncertainty. The system pieces were also stretched beyond their normal situational limits. It wasn't clear how they would behave; there was no precedent.

Deciding to affect a big part of a complex system also can't be based solely on its current demands. The assumption must be that things will change. Exponential growth was an example assumption that disease history supported. Yet a complete understanding of future conditions is impossible for unprecedented situations that affect complex systems. Decisions must be made with monkey wrenches and adaptability in mind.

For many years, I worked with a part of the U.S. military that plans movement of everything from dignitaries to toilet paper. It turns out that scheduling lots of trips is a favorite math problem known for having so many possibilities that finding an optimal solution can be unlikely...even with powerful computers. That's true when the objective is well defined, but it's made even harder because "best" is debatable. Is "best" getting everything from A to B as quickly as possible? If so then the cost will be higher (e.g., aircraft move things faster but cost more than ships). Safety also factors in. Some of the possible air routes would pass over places unwelcoming to the U.S. military. "Best" will change meaning depending on the situational context.

Then there's the short-term versus long-term tradeoff. Perhaps something near the optimum trip pattern (a trip being a plan with a schedule, vehicle, routes, cargo, etc.) can be found for the near-term needs. However, it could put the vehicles in a poorly distributed pattern to adjust to a future surprise. It could be effective but not easily adaptable. The field of robust optimization seeks to elevate adaptability as a core criterion for "best."

That's how hard it is to deal with complex systems when the people in the system are doing what they are told to do; presumably military personnel follow their directions. Put in some less cooperative or mysterious entities and finding "best" becomes less a computational challenge and more an art form. It becomes something only a combination of machines and people can effectively solve.

I've explained how every job will change and some will disappear or become unrecognizable. I've indicated that wisdom skills are more important than expertise skills in the AI era, and that there are indications that wisdom is scarce in the population.

This chapter explores where the increased demand for wisdom originates. It's not all from AI. After all, the 21st-Century Skills were outlined a couple of decades ago as a response to a changing world. Business has long been asking for more teamwork, innovation, and critical thinking that are driven by wisdom as much or more than expertise. Why does the world need more wisdom? Answering that question should inform the educational response.

I place the onus on increasing complexity. The more interconnected our world becomes, the more we analyze problems across institutional and disciplinary boundaries, and the more we try to affect or are captive to the thinking of people—the more complex many jobs have become.

I want to distinguish complex from complicated. To many scientists, those are two different things.[57]

Complicated systems are made up of lots of pieces, but each part can be designed or solved on its own. A complicated system could be put into a giant block diagram, with each block a separate, solvable piece. Moreover, one can control a complicated system's behavior and assume it will behave the same at every future time. We can analyze complicated systems with models and control them with rules or set processes. Since the time of the Industrial Revolution, we have dramatically improved our ability to build reliable complicated systems... largely because of expertise.

Complex systems are a different beast. They have lots of factors that will affect how they behave, as with complicated systems, but those factors are so intertwined, uncertain, and time-varying that predicting the behavior of the system from some intervention is always imprecise. It's even hard to define where one complex system ends and another begins. Complex systems can have emergent properties that aren't predictable from the individual pieces, like with beehives, life-form evolution, the social Internet, and most modern AI. As the scientist and educator Donella Meadows indicates, "The behavior of a system cannot be known just by knowing the elements of which the system is made."[58] The goals of complicated systems can be written down in specifications. For complex systems the goals and even problem statements are debatable.

Complex systems require wisdom. If they're treated by leaders as complicated problems instead, then significant dangers arise.[59] They may try to solve a problem when managing it is more realistic. Leaders could assume a one-time intervention will suffice versus having the humility to understand that an iterative, adaptive approach is more applicable. They might wish away influences they can't control or fail to recognize them at all.

Whether with COVID-19, military transportation, or workplace jobs, it is increasingly hard to break up problems and solutions into independent or single-discipline tasks. Each person affecting the system should ideally understand many perspectives on what might or should happen.

"Whew," you may say. "Lucky that's not my job." Ah...but it likely is. In the 20th century...the era of physics, chemistry, factory optimization, and the mechanical...a typical job plugged into a giant complicated system (the company) to produce something tangible. Fairly few people were involved in free-thinking cognitive activities. Company departments operated more independently, with coordination consisting of throwing information "over the fence." Labor was often doing the same thing repeatedly whether in the factory or the office. Work was within a complicated system with labor fitting into well-defined blocks in the system diagram.

Companies now have complexity problems. Business is global. Information floods. Pesky, uncertain human beings drive the behavior of systems, including the ones at a company. Companies can't tease apart marketing, sales, development, and research to the degree they once could. People who have skills that bridge silos are the diamonds. All because there is more complexity in the world.

The need for wisdom arises from that complexity, independent of AI's advancement. AI just turbocharges it. It accelerates what has been a long-term trend. Workers need not only to be wise, but to be wise about much more complex problems than dealt with by prior generations.

In this chapter I discuss three intellectual needs associated with modern complexity: increasingly abstract thinking, finding meaning and truth in bigger information piles, and handling more uncertainty.

INCREASING ABSTRACTION

Considering something more abstractly is a process of conceptualizing an idea, heuristic, rule, or generalization from the detail or examples at a lower abstraction level. The opposite of an abstraction is a specification. Abstractions necessarily throw out information but are often needed so we don't overload our limited ability to simultaneously consider many pieces. An effective abstraction preserves the ability to predict something while allowing manipulation of fewer information pieces.

As the next chapter will discuss in more detail, at any point there are two cognitive ways to go. One can drill down into more detail (specify) or consider bigger-picture principles (abstractify). We often jump back and forth between those thinking modes, but they are very difficult to consider simultaneously.

Both complex and complicated systems contain too much information for conscious mental manipulation. Decades of research on how much information people can hold in their heads at once show that we are quite limited. That so-called working memory can hold a very small number of information pieces, depending on the person and the type of information. Fortunately, the information pieces in working memory can be at any abstraction level. The more complicated or complex a system, the more our brains need to use abstraction.

You may think computerization is responsible for the higher abstraction imperative, and it surely has contributed, but the trend seems to go back further. James Flynn studied Intelligence Quotient (IQ) test results spanning many decades...at first to refute one researcher who claimed lower IQ scores from minorities was evidence of genetic differences between races.[60] Flynn analyzed the data and found just the opposite. IQ scores seem more related to environment than genetics.

What he noticed is that IQ scores have increased in the developed world since at least 1900.[61] It's such a big effect that an American with an IQ score of 100 (average) in 1900 would only score a 67 in 2000, which in modern parlance would be considered cognitively impaired.[62] Since humanity surely didn't genetically evolve much in that time, the difference must be due to nurture...not nature. The growth of IQ in successive generations is now called the Flynn Effect.

The Flynn Effect wasn't obvious because IQ test results are adjusted so that the average for every age group in every year is 100. The intent is a comparison with peers. Flynn looked at the raw scores before they were adjusted for year and age.

IQ tests are an understandable third-rail topic for many. IQ's have been used to justify greatly harmful and inaccurate attitudes about the innate ability of various segments of society. They have been used to screen in discriminatory ways. The original intent of IQ tests—to define an unchanging and comprehensive intellectual capacity of a person—was not accomplished. IQ is neither unchanging nor comprehensive. Test performance can and does change throughout one's life, and...on average...from grandma to us. Lots of important human qualities don't get measured in IQ tests. Despite that checkered history, IQ measures are useful indications of general cognitive abilities that are correlated with performance in school and career.[63]

Digging even further into the data reveals that the Flynn Effect is especially from improvement in abstract thinking and problem solving. IQ tests show us becoming better abstract thinkers. The reason for this trend is debated. Flynn himself thought people were learning abstract thinking better because the world presents more abstraction than it used to (as I too am claiming). Other explanations include better education, nutrition, child-rearing, or test-taking skills. The likely explanation is some combination.

The increasing need for abstract thinking because of AI is evident in the ways we must interact with it. Using ChatGPT, for example, requires several increased abstractions. Human generation of text...already an abstract activity...is replaced by even more abstract skills that decide how to ask for text and judge the veracity and usefulness of the output.

The implications for schooling are clear. If abstractness is a necessary cognitive characteristic for dealing with complex systems, and if more work involves interactions with or design of complex systems, then what is taught to students must also rise to greater abstraction levels. Each abstraction level is different and has its own competency.

Consider math instruction, for example. In many classes, students still learn and use many equations, are taught to derive math theorems, and learn detailed methods for manually solving problems. The problem is those talents have limited utility in the real world. Studies show that most people have little need to use the math skills they are taught in high school. As of 2013, fewer than a quarter of U.S. workers reported using math in their jobs beyond the percentages and fractions they learned about in middle school.[64] Interestingly, blue-collar tradespeople use more math than white-collar workers.

The argument that solving an equation by hand is useful in real life may have been true for some future scientists in the moon-launch era, but it's not true now. Workers don't solve math tasks by hand. Computers solve them, and we often don't teach the computer methods. Schools also ignore major math topics that are more important now than during moon launches. Statistics, for example, is critical for information analysis that dominates today's workplaces, but calculus is still the high school priority. Calculus is more important for the design of mechanical things.

Workers now need to understand when math might help, choose an appropriate method, and properly interpret the output of computer processing. Those are entirely different skills that have little in common with manually applying a formula. In the future—when AI can choose the type of math for us and perhaps explain the proper interpretation—then the human contribution will be even more abstract. We will have to pose problems and questions in ways that inform AI about the best choice of math.

I get a lot of interesting responses when I bring up the decreasing value of some forms of math instruction. Many educators and parents express surprise. They assume others must need the math even if they don't. Others acknowledge the issue but default to an argument about math helping general logic or problem-solving skills. Great—those are transferable skills (ones that are useful across expertise domains). The problem is if that is really the goal, then I can think of much more wholistic ways to teach those skills. Otherwise, schools are teaching only an aspect of logic having to do with math operations that lead to single, precise answers. The college professors I know indicate many students aren't demonstrating sound logic or problem-solving skills. They report that students often plug numbers into equations and crank out answers without understanding what it all means. Time spent solving problems by hand obscures the conceptual takeaways needed to adapt to real-world challenges.

Even professional scientists may not have a strong enough conceptual grasp. For example, there is evidence that the scientifically trained don't entirely understand the most common test for statistical significance—the p-value. That measure is often used as the sole indicator of whether an experiment proves or disproves something.

I'm not going to go into details of p-value misuse—I don't want to put you into a coma—but it has gotten so bad that more than 800 prominent mathematicians have recently endorsed banning the measure.[65] In an analysis of almost 800 research papers across five different fields (not related to the 800 signatories of this view) they showed half of the authors misinterpreted p-value. The problem isn't that the measure is a bad one, but it's only one way of understanding uncertain information. It shouldn't be used on its own to declare certainty of success or failure of a hypothesis. That's a conceptually blind application of math that I think is an outcome of too much emphasis on outdated math-solving mechanics—and too little on what the math is doing to help life's challenges.

The nature of needs for reading and writing has also changed. The rise of AI that can read and write changes human needs. People can have virtually anything read to them in audio form. They can now have much of the core writing done for them. The utility of reading and writing is lower—or at least different. There should be an expanded emphasis on editing, fact-checking, and skimming of written material to purposely extract some information at the exclusion of others.

Don't misinterpret what I'm saying. Please continue to teach reading, writing, and math, but pay close attention to how the use conditions are different. We must teach the higher abstraction skills.

What then is the right balance?

Can people learn to select the appropriate math without knowing how to prove or solve an equation? Yes...I think so. Those skills seem largely independent from one another.

Can people edit AI-generated text well without being excellent readers and writers? That's less clear. From my coding days I know that being able to modify someone else's software was easier to do than writing it from scratch. Code modification is a step in the software engineer's learning process. Maybe writing instruction won't need to go much farther than that step.

Education has orthodoxies like any other field. One is the belief that there are knowledge prerequisites to learning new knowledge, and that abstractions can't be learned without the underlying knowledge. However, the research shows the power of prior knowledge in various learning studies to be almost nil, though with high variability.[66] Prior knowledge isn't sufficient. Psychologist Garvin Brod says there are three requirements needed for prior knowledge to have learning impact.[67] It must be activated—unremembered knowledge can't help. The knowledge must be relevant to the current task. Finally, the old knowledge must be congruent with what must be learned; we have a hard time learning new information that doesn't mesh with our prior knowledge and mindset.

I also think we need to be careful about how well prior research centered on expertise-learning assumptions will apply to wisdom learning. Those two aspects of intellect operate on different principles...as I will lay out later...and learn differently. Most of the educational experiments judge learning based on retention of detailed knowledge or narrow, domain-specific concepts—expertise stuff. Experiments typically test participant learning of factual details, not abstract notions.

It is obvious that not all abstraction levels need to be taught to learn a higher-level idea. Making decisions about human health doesn't require knowing the electron states of atoms. Anticipating how human behavior might affect a complex piece of software doesn't require knowing exactly how the software is coded, nor the life story of each user. Some knowledge is important, but not all knowledge at all abstraction levels. It's also not clear how much of the knowledge needs to be omnipresent in our brains versus supplied on-demand by the Internet or AI.

Higher complexity and AI both require thinking at increasingly abstract levels. Schools must focus on teaching to higher abstraction.

BIGGER HAYSTACKS

Another aspect of complex systems in the modern age is that critical information can be lost in an increasingly ginormous pile of extraneous information.

When I was a child, a big and common family purchase was an encyclopedia. It usually came in several volumes with incremental updates in yearly tomes...physical ones. It was our Internet of the day, supplemented by Walter Cronkite (famous news anchor) and his competitors at the two other TV stations, and of course a trip to the local library or museum. It took a long time to find out about something, and there were far fewer sources to consider.

Now knowledge is so plentiful that we're drowning in it. It is estimated that the average American consumed five times as much information in 2008 as they did in 1980.[68] That number went up another 20% between 2011 and 2021.[69] The information pile grew even faster. Our ability to consume more information will never catch up to the growth and accessibility of it. Humans can remember an increasingly vanishing fraction of the world's information.

That change means our information strategy must be different. By analogy, if you lived in a time and place where water is scarce—before indoor plumbing—then capture and storage were the critical needs. You'd drink what you can get. When information was scarcer and time consuming to get, then remembering it was critical. If there's a big body of drinking water nearby, then scarcity is no longer the issue. Getting the water to where it's needed and determining if it's safe become more important. When we're drowning in information, the ability to select and verify it is paramount.

This has many effects on how we seek and consume information. It pushes us toward skimming rather than slow, deep reading. In graduate school I remember latching onto a few key AI papers that I reread many times. Then again, there were orders of magnitude fewer AI papers, and my research had a narrow focus. Now I need to get pieces of information from a lot of different places. I skim research papers. I may read the abstract and the findings and recommendations. If those are relevant to me, only then will I jump to the methods and judge whether the work was done in a proper way. Reading comprehension in my childhood was often defined as whether I would remember something in a body of text after reading it. These days...in a work context...it should be measured by how quickly I can find information relevant to my reading purpose and understand to what degree it might be correct.

There are many who bemoan the loss of deep reading and what that does to our thinking processes.[70] However, that change isn't inherently bad. Like most adaptations, it trades one advantage for another. It's a logical reaction to information overflow. Skimming is purposeful reading meant to grab the most relevant pieces and move on. Perhaps you are skimming this book. We are adapting to a new reality. There used to be only so much information on a subject. Now it's practically infinite.

We aren't going to stop the information flood; we can't wish it away. People must have the knowledge to do efficient information search and discovery and the judgment skills to suspect when information may be misleading or incorrect. ′

RISING UNCERTAINTY

Horst Rittel was a German-born professor who for thirty years specialized in design. Unlike what that term may connote in a modern work context, he wasn't working on product aesthetics or usability. Rather, he was a design theorist, deep into methods and practices for designing complex systems...especially in social system planning.

His training was in math and physics, so he brought a scientific and numerical experience base to the work. By the late 60s, he was seeing that scientific approaches to social planning were failing.

Rittel and his colleague Melvin Webber at the University of California at Berkeley reframed the design challenge. In a landmark philosophical paper in 1973, Rittel and Webber defined the notion of wicked problems.[71] They weren't using the term wicked to mean evil. Nor were they adopting New England slang, where wicked can mean "extremely" or "excellent." Instead, the term contrasted with "tame" or "benign" problems that science most often tackled.

They specified ten attributes of wicked problems in social policy. Later, Dr. Jeffrey Conklin shortened the list to six points, generalizing to wicked problems beyond social policy. Those are:[72]

1. "The problem is not understood until after the formulation of a solution.
2. Wicked problems have no stopping rule.
3. Solutions to wicked problems are not right or wrong.
4. Every wicked problem is essentially novel and unique.
5. Every solution to a wicked problem is a 'one shot operation'.
6. Wicked problems have no given alternative solutions."

At the heart of wicked problems is tremendous uncertainty—not only about the system and solutions to problems, but also about the problem itself.

There is much confusion about the notion of wicked problems, so let me again use the COVID-19 pandemic as an example. It clearly fits the definition.

The pandemic was a unique event. The problem had never been addressed, in that the conditions for prior events were always different (#4). There is no chance to learn by trial-and-error (#5). The quality of solutions to the pandemic is a function of the values one places on the multiple kinds of outcomes (e.g., disease propagation, economic conditions). There is no absolute right or wrong (#3), but rather better or worse, with best being different for each human judge.

The three remaining wicked problem criteria are a bit more difficult to understand. The pandemic clearly isn't a chess game where the decision maker understands when and how well the job has been accomplished. No matter what was accomplished in responding to the pandemic, we could always have done better. If the decision maker stops doing things, it's because they have "run out of time, money, or patience."[71] COVID-19 is still around, but we stop treating it the same way because of those external pressures (#2). Criterion #6 doesn't mean there are no alternative solutions, but rather that there are always solutions that aren't thought of. It is a matter of judgment and creativity which solution is pursued. The decision maker can be more or less informed, but what to do about it isn't clearly mapped from information to solution. Finally, and perhaps most attributable to wicked systems, the problem and the solution are intertwined (#1). There is no definitive statement of the problem; people can disagree about it. Potential solutions reveal new aspects of the problem or create new problems. Rittel said "One cannot understand the problem without knowing about its context; one cannot meaningfully search for information without the orientation of a solution concept; one cannot first understand, then solve."[71]

At the heart of wicked problems is the uncertainty inherent in complex systems. A big part of that is because human beings are key parts of the system being perturbed, and human behavior is always uncertain.

Wicked problems aren't only global ones. Workers are in a wicked problem decision space when they are devising a marketing approach, a corporate strategy, or performing a variety of other everyday roles. In those situations, many perspectives must be shared because there is no definitive answer. Heck...there's no definitive problem. Those are different kinds of challenges than optimizing the productivity of a factory floor, where the goal is often to reduce the variability of worker behavior.

Science tries to reduce uncertainty. I looked up quotes related to complexity for the beginning of this chapter and was drowned in ones that say some form of "complexity is easy; it's harder to make something simple." I get the point. It's important to be able to explain something in easily understandable terms. Simplicity can't be the goal though. It can't be used to wish away complexity.

We educate people on subjects that have laws that drive system behavior. After a while it can seem that every subject has laws. True complex systems don't have laws that are invariant to context. They can't be effectively dealt with by oversimplifications. My COVID-19 gut was educated but oversimplified. I had neglected the more uncertain aspects of the system over the parts that I understood.

We have the tendency to try to reduce uncertainty...to simplify tasks until the pathway is clear. Complex systems have inherent uncertainty. People have to deal with it—not bury it. Education needs to embrace it.

§

The world is more complex. That seems partly due to a dramatic increase in how much we can know given an explosion of discovery and creation. There's good and bad to it. The more information there is, the higher the likelihood that something can be analyzed. We can ask more questions, have more ideas, make more discoveries, and create more solutions.

It isn't only that information begets more information. The systems are inherently more complex. Most human history had us interacting with a relatively isolated set of people, in a culture that changed little across generations, and in a natural environment that at best could be locally known and influenced. Now humanity is global, and that increased complexity emphasizes different skills. Those skills rely on increasingly abstract thinking in settings that are drowning in information and have more uncertainty.

I have said I am not anti-expertise, but rather that the balance between wisdom and expertise must be reset. I know that knowledge still matters a great deal. The question is: which knowledge.

In a world with more complexity, the key knowledge is at a higher abstraction level. The superforecasters didn't usually know about the domains they were forecasting in. Rather, they applied meta-knowledge (knowledge about knowledge) about information gathering and vetting, decision making, and analysis processes.

It is a big sign of a tepid commitment to 21st-Century Skills that there are not required courses on those skills. People can be taught the knowledge of critical thinking, which could include how people make decisions, how to interpret statistical information, signals of veracity and doubt, and processes for mitigating cognitive biases. There is a rich body of knowledge around interpersonal interaction and the considerations for persuading, negotiating, counseling, and detecting personality indicators. The subject of complex systems is itself well studied. Knowledge is still important, but the nature of our challenges is now different. So too must be the key knowledge.

Schooling is caught in the middle. They tout the new-age skills but largely don't teach the new-age knowledge, which will tend to be more abstract, involve ways to sort through lots of information, and require dealing with greater uncertainty. There is reluctance to add to an already overloaded curriculum, but that's because subtractions are usually not considered.

Half-way hasn't worked...and it won't.

As the next few chapters describe, learning wisdom requires a very different approach, one nearly upside down from traditional instruction.

4.

THE ROOTS OF WISDOM

*The intuitive mind is a sacred gift and the rational mind is a
faithful servant. We have created a society that honors the
servant and has forgotten the gift.*

Albert Einstein[73]

"She's doing this all in her head," my colleague whispered.
"Amazing."

We were in a nondescript conference room observing several epidemiologists from a public health department play a game.

The game task was to identify a terrorist cell rehearsing an airport attack by piecing together many threads of evidence.[74] The hypothetical terrorists weren't attacking with a disease, but we thought we could adapt the game to a disease investigation application. Having the public health folks play the security game would stimulate brain cells for discussion about an outbreak detection game.

Epidemiologists are not police, but we learned disease detectives might be pretty good at catching terrorists.

The premise was that something odd was discovered in a checked bag—not an illegal something, but an unusual something suggestive of malicious intent. Each team had to find the potential actors and were scored by speed, completeness, and accuracy. We simulated stories of the people in the airport including flight check-in records, criminal databases, license plates of vehicles, phone records, etc. In that haystack was a terrorist cell rehearsing for an attack. The checked bag anomaly was the first clue.

Players got dribbles of information over time, like in real life, and their jobs were to find more of the cell using various data sources. There were a lot of subtle clues to string together. For example, if John and Sally drove to the airport separately but live together, then they might have different travel schedules or may be masking their association. If either one is discovered to be affiliated with a suspected cell member, then both could be suspect. There were a lot of these "maybe" clues.

The game was meant to be a tool for us researchers. We wanted to understand inefficient or intellectually difficult parts of decision processes that technology might help. The airport game was played by eleven teams of three people: two with MIT scientists, eight with police and/or security, and one of disease hunters from public health.

The lead of the public health team was keeping all the threads and potential linkages in her head. All the other teams wrote down the clues. It became a lot for one skull. That's what my colleague was commenting on. The epidemiologists nevertheless made timely, effective decisions.

When team scores were compared, MIT scientists were two of the three worst performing teams while the public health team was fourth best—better than some police teams.75 There's nothing statistically meaningful to report with this data, but I intuited meaning behind the scores. In doing so I'm committing scientific heresy, at least for some parts of the community where qualitative observations or philosophical musing is behaviorally discouraged. Yet I think such suspicions, if understood as speculative, can be very powerful drivers of innovation.

Intuition has lost street cred. It is the fast-thinking, unconscious cognition that makes most of our decisions. It is the engine of insight, the wellspring of "aha," and the fount of "wait a minute."

If I asked players how they made game judgments, or even the mental process they used, I doubt I'd get a cogent answer. Intuition isn't lingual, but that doesn't mean it's uninformed.

The public health team, like the police ones, seemed more fluid doing the work and taking roles than the MIT teams. There was something about connect-the-dots investigative work that seemed to transcend disease-digging and be relevant in transportation security. They were better at something in another domain than it seemed they should be, unless their intuition about investigations in general could power both realms (or...of course...unless that team was a statistical anomaly). I had intuition about their intuition.

This chapter describes the fundamentals of wisdom in the brain, and the next chapter explains how it is acquired. Intuition is a critical ingredient.

Another brain aspect is also essential. At the risk of eye-rolling, I've got to talk about the brain hemispheres. While it doesn't map perfectly, the orientations of the brain hemispheres are related to the empowering attributes of expertise and wisdom respectively. The right brain's wisdom orientation is powered by multi-use, abstract concepts that power intuition. As future chapters will describe, we learn that very differently than expertise.

THE OTHER LEFT AND RIGHT

Consider the following thought experiment. One person wants to poison their boss but fails to because he mistakenly uses sugar instead of rat poison. Another person accidentally kills his boss by unknowingly giving poison instead of sugar. Which is morally superior?

Most healthy brains would say the person who intended to kill was more immoral...regardless of the outcome...versus having no intention to kill. We enforce that morality in society as well. Attempted murder is a more serious charge in the U.S. than is involuntary manslaughter.

The answers were very different for individuals who had the connection between their brain hemispheres severed. Those split-brain patients had the radical procedure as a last resort treatment for severe epilepsy. Over several decades, they supplied some of the most interesting neurological insights of our time. Roger Sperry—the originator of split-brain research—earned a Nobel Prize in 1981 for his work.

Michael Gazzaniga studied under Roger Sperry in the 60s at the California Institute of Technology and continued split-brain research throughout his professorial career. It was he, his student, and a few other collaborators who were posing the rat poison moral comparison to both split and unsplit brains in the late-00s.

The results were clear; the split-brain patients, across several such stories, judged morality by the outcome—not the belief of intentionality.[76] They usually said the accidental death of the boss was morally inferior.

What is it about severing the relatively small neural connection highway (the corpus callosum) between the left and right cerebral cortexes that completely alters typical moral judgment?

Sperry and Gazzaniga's experiments have shown that we have two brains that act mostly independently with a low-bandwidth connection between them. The left hemisphere senses from and moves the right side of the body, and the right hemisphere does so with the left body. Researchers can use that division in split-brain patients to challenge each hemisphere independently.

Many split-brain experiments focused on language and visual interpretation. For example, a word might be shown to only the left or right side of the visual field. If a split-brain patient is asked what word was shown, the left brain can readily answer. The right brain cannot.[77]

It is because of language and the prevalence of right-handedness that the left brain was long considered the dominant side. In the early 1900s, speech production and language understanding areas were found in the left hemisphere. There was seemingly no counterpart to those regions in the right hemisphere. Later, other intellectual qualities like logic and abstraction were also attributed to the left brain. It became vogue to assume the left brain was in charge, clearly with "more important" roles like language and the ability to control our better hand.

Split-brain research showed the right hemisphere understood language after all. If the right brain of a split-brain patient is shown a word, then the person can't repeat it but can draw a picture of it. One experiment showed the word "girlfriend" to the right hemisphere of a split-brain teenage subject known as P.S. (for anonymization). He nonverbally indicated with a head shake and a shrug that he didn't see any word. Then he chuckled. He reached out with his left hand—controlled by the right brain—and lined up three of the Scrabble tiles in front of him. He spelled L-I-Z...his girlfriend's name.[78] His right brain could understand language after all; it just didn't have the means to speak.

The right brain is involved in most of the same functions that the left brain is...although in a very different way. Scientists now know that functions that were thought to lie only in the left hemisphere also have a home in the right.

The press was hyperbolic about split-brain research. The right hemisphere was the artistic and creative side...so the stories went... while the left was the scientific and logical part. So much shlock science followed that it became career suicide for researchers to study hemispheric differences. It has only been in the last decade or so that the taint has dissolved.

Even now, I enter this discussion with caution. You undoubtedly already have preconceived notions about the left and right brains, and they're probably more wrong than right. The left brain isn't the scientific side and the right the artistic or creative one. As science currently understands it, those characterizations are inaccurate. The education world is inundated with so-called right-brain learning techniques to teach things like creativity. Creativity—or critical thinking, or communication, or whatever complex brain activity you can think of— needs both hemispheres for peak operation.

The confusion is understandable given how even neuroscientists often speak about brain function. It's worth a bit of a tangent to explain how brain function can be difficult to interpret. I'll be back to right and left brain in a few paragraphs.

Neuroscience has long tried to understand what function the parts of the brain are performing. That's a difficult endeavor—one that can have a very different answer at one abstraction level, or in one set of conditions, than for another.

A brain region is a physically organized collection of neurons that transmit and transform other neuron signals. Science can't yet measure every neuron's firing. Instead, they measure macroscopic changes in a person's behavior or physiology that result from the pattern of neuron firings in a brain region.

There are a few ways to observe the relationship between a brain region and a function. For more than a century, the changes in abilities or behaviors from naturally occurring brain injury (e.g., strokes, physical injury) were noted. If the injury affected speech, for example, then the region of the injury must be involved in speech. Modern methods can help analyze presumably uninjured brains too. Functional imaging methods show time-evolving maps of the blood flow in brain regions—blood flow being correlated with neuron firing activity. New brain stimulation technology can change the activity level in regions of the cerebral cortex (responsible for most of what we call thinking) without cracking open the skull. Clues are generated about the involvement of a brain region in a function by measuring brain activity during particular tasks.

Functional characterization of the brain has nevertheless been challenged by many complications that can lead to misinterpretation.

No two brains are physically alike. No two people have the same experiences. The same region can have different functions in different people. Brain regions compete with one another. If one brain region isn't being used much—like with the blind or deaf—then other functions will expand into that turf. Those differences mean many people are needed for statistical characterization of results. Plus, there are a ton of things to give a brain to do. The different types of experimental methods and research subjects make it difficult to compare research.

Neuroscientists try to explain what they think their data means. That brings them into the realm of vague, imperfect language. Their interpretations can be infused with philosophical and other biases.

The challenge asked of a brain can bias the functional explanation. If one region is implicated in math calculations, then it can be incorrectly labeled a math region, but it may have a more versatile role...like in symbolic manipulation...that can only be seen through more varied challenges. After all, math is a relatively new need on the long timeline of human history; it's unlikely to have gotten dedicated genetic resources.

Let me give an example. The cerebellum is a brain region at the back of our skulls that contains over half of the neurons in the entire brain. It is usually described as responsible for fine motor coordination since damage to it results in movement incoordination.

There are at least two biases that conclusion represents.

The first is the lamppost problem. We are more likely to find our lost keys where there is light...under the lamppost. Some brain functions are easier to notice, and experiments are designed around those functions. We see muscles contract. We don't directly observe another person's abstract internal thoughts. The experimental choices drive what is discovered.

The second bias is that the brain is divided up according to the ways we categorize observable behaviors. That philosophy infuses data interpretations. If we believe some portions of the brain are exclusively for motor function, then that will infuse experimental explanations versus a more abstract or multi-functional purpose.

That seems the case for the cerebellum. Recent research shows it is also involved in more abstract thinking, emotion, and other body signal processing.[79] The brain seemingly maps many concepts to the same...or similar...circuits that control muscle movement. It seems the cerebellum is applying the same general concept to different forms of data because its neural network structure is similar throughout.

So then is the cerebellum really about movement coordination, or is it multi-functional and driven by more abstract considerations? Both psychological and AI research point to the latter. One theory is that the cerebellum may be the place that reinforcement learning happens—one of the major modes of human and AI learning.[80]

Reinforcement learning uses errors in the interpretation of the world as feedback for improvement. The cerebellum could be analogous to a software subroutine that's used whenever reinforcement learning is needed.

The roles of the two brain hemispheres have been similarly confused. The more obvious behaviors...the ones easier to design experiments for...are often testing left brain strengths. As a result, the right brain was historically considered weak and relatively unimportant.

In the latter part of the 20th century, understanding of the right brain changed.[81,82] It became understood as the place for key forms of visual and spatial processing such as face recognition. It does a lot of nonverbal communication and sensing. It has a stronger tie to our emotions. It has a key role in storytelling, analogizing, and deciphering meaning. It tries more to understand people.

Yet those too are attributes of the system, not its purpose. To really understand what the hemispheres are all about we need to consider why there are hemispheres at all.

Studies of brain evolution strongly suggest the hemisphere distinctions must be important for survival. Lateralized neural processing is a vertebrate staple.[83] Animals that have gone down very different evolutionary paths, like birds and apes, each have hemispheres. The two sides are physically different—as with humans. That's even true of nerve clumps in invertebrates.[84]

Maybe there are two sides to processing because there are two sides to the body? That seems an unlikely explanation. It's not clear why a dividing line between the left and right body is necessary versus a gradual transition. It makes evolving a third hand much harder! Evolution can make mistakes. It could result in attributes that no longer serve a useful purpose, but it's hard to believe brain asymmetry would have survived in such a pervasive way unless there is a big advantage.

The hemispheres are anatomically different, suggesting they aren't designed to do the same jobs.[85] They are not the same size and shape. The left hemisphere has more volume, and more of it in the back of the skull. The right hemisphere has more volume in the frontal lobe than the left. The left hemisphere has a noticeable bulge on the left side of the head corresponding to language areas unique to our species of ape. The hemispheres are even twisted a bit around each other (the Yaklovian torque) in an apparent attempt to find the room for these asymmetries. Left and right brains have different connection patterns, with the right brain having more long-distance nerves that connect diverse brain centers.[86] The left hemisphere's connections tend to be more local.

Curiously, it may be the competition between the hemispheres... across their connecting link...that could keep them specialized.[87] Kim Peek—the now deceased savant who was the basis for the Raymond Babbitt character in the movie *Rain Man*—had a genetic condition that resulted in the lack of a corpus callosum. His two cortical hemispheres were not connected. One of the apparent results of this disconnection is that he developed typically left-brain capabilities in both hemispheres. For example, he could read both pages of an open book at the same time, with the left page being read by the left eye and the right page by the right eye.[88] However...as the movie indicated...other brain functions were more difficult for him, especially those typically associated with the right brain.

What is it then? Why do we have two brain hemispheres?

Our modern understanding of the roles of the two hemispheres is well described in Iain McGilchrist's book *The Master and his Emissary*.[89] The title speaks to a brain hemisphere allegory. The master (right brain) sends his emissary (left brain) on errands requiring specialized skills. The emissary does the errand and reports back to the master who can integrate what was learned or accomplished into the overall goals. Contrary to historical bias, McGilchrist puts the right brain in charge.

The world presents a choice to a brain—either drill down into more detail to illuminate mechanisms or to build something to fix a problem, or take a more wholistic view, stepping back to assess whether all the relevant information has been accessed and if there is a greater principle that should guide thinking and action. Those two paradigms need their separation. Pursuing either one comes at the cost of the other. They are both necessary to understand the world, but can't be done together, at the same time, in the same neural circuits. The hemispheres are evidently driven by different ways of understanding the world. Some birds, for example, do the detailed work to pick out food with their right eye (controlled by the left hemisphere) while looking out for predators with their left eye (controlled by the right hemisphere).[90]

The hemisphere differences are most often described as detail-oriented (left) versus whole-oriented (right)—which jives with my expertise and wisdom distinctions.

My AI experience tells me that the hemisphere differentiation should be a result of different learning emphases. The brain is a learning engine. Its ability to adapt is perhaps its chief characteristic. The question in my mind is what criteria the hemispheres are using to learn. Just as an AI will try to optimize something as it learns, so too might a brain hemisphere. Therefore, asking what the hemispheres do functionally may not be as important as asking what they are trying to optimize.

The left brain seems to try to minimize uncertainty in its interpretation of the world.[91] That optimization goal should drive it to focus on details, especially ones that can be precisely defined and controlled. Examining detail was for most of human history useful in interacting with the inanimate or natural world. Detail was critical to distinguish edible from poisonous, for example, or to create and use the most effective tool. Detail work requires precision and memory for facts. The left brain can manipulate fine detail—like for making tools—since it has access to the usually more adept right hand. Control and manipulation are personality characteristics associated with the left brain. It is strong at focused attention...the kind that details need. An uncertainty minimization purpose also suggests dismissal of aspects that are inherently uncertain like the behaviors of other human beings.

In contrast, the right brain appears to try to maximize the completeness and consistency of its world observations.[91] It has an unfocused attention that's on the lookout for novelty and meaning. It is sensitive to context, intents, consequences, and lessons. Since it's relatively unphased by uncertainty, a well-functioning right brain has the raw materials to make wise interpersonal choices. The right side is where mental models of self and others lie. Most of our nuanced emotions are processed in the right hemisphere. It accounts for meaning, metaphor, and humor. Unlike the left brain's explicit language, much of what the right brain knows can't easily be articulated. It is a more intuitive hemisphere.

The left hemisphere will break a human interaction down into parts, for example, but fitting the pieces back together doesn't readily lead to a whole that makes sense. The whole is its own thing, distinct from the assemblage of parts.

In contrast, the right hemisphere is about the whole, the gestalt, the big picture. For example, the right brain can learn to recognize that another person is exhibiting a certain emotion. That requires simultaneous recognition of many subtle clues. The left hemisphere can see an eyebrow is raised and the mouth is agape, but it doesn't readily put those signs into a more wholistic context—that a person may be surprised. The right brain can't talk, so its abilities can seem more gut feel than rationale. The left hemisphere will have to describe what the right hemisphere is understanding...a translation that might not go well.

Consider again the allegory about the master (left brain) and its emissary (right brain). The master delegates specific and more detailed work to the emissary. The emissary is given autonomy, but that can backfire. The emissary never sees the full scope of what the master must deal with. Over time the emissary could come to believe he could do the master's job. The master doesn't explain to the emissary the other responsibilities—or potentially why she's tasking the emissary the way he does. The emissary doesn't see the other aspects of the boss' work, and the master doesn't have the specialty skills to do what the emissary can.

The left brain—the emissary—can thus be deluded. It knows only the pieces of the world it is tasked to analyze, but not the big picture. So...it invents its own. In the rat poison thought experiment, the left brain of each split-brain subject was the only side that could speak, and it couldn't get an explanation from the right brain. The left brain's answer is utilitarian (outcome-focused) because it is not in its arsenal to deal with the nuances of morality or to tradeoff intent and outcome.

Perhaps the biggest difference in an expertise-oriented view of the world and a wisdom-inclined one is that they are driven by different hemispheres—expertise by the left, and wisdom by the right. This isn't an esoteric point. It matters because those two sides learn very differently. There is a parallel between the left brain and the detail-oriented, analytical, and overconfident experts, and between the right brain and the big-picture, storytelling, teaming, and humble super-forecasters.

Neither the expert nor the sage start life that way. They become according to how they are incubated. In our society, brains are bathed in detail and lightly rinsed with big picture. Considerable effort is expended to develop left-brain, expertise-oriented skills. The right-brain, wisdom-oriented skills are relatively neglected, and sometimes actively dismissed.

Our society favors the development of expertise, so it's logical that left brains will be better developed. One could hope that wisdom comes with expertise development, but it's hard to generate wholistic insight from looking at many pieces. The big-picture path is a different one.

It's important to understand that the hemisphere characterizations represent typical properties, but there is tremendous individual variation. Functions normally undertaken by one side might be done by the other, though perhaps less optimally (e.g., fewer long-range connections in the left brain may limit how big picture it can get). Most importantly, the brain is use-it-or-lose-it. Deny a brain the fuel for wisdom and expertise functions might expand into its turf.

There is no either-or in this discussion. Both hemispheres are used all the time, and exchange information on microsecond time scales. Both are critical. The question is how good they are at their jobs. Left-brain expertise has the upper hand because it is the emphasis of society, education, and work structure.

The ramifications of a left-brain overemphasis are on display in many work settings.

LEFT-BRAIN WORK ENVIRONMENTS

Once you absorb the implications of the two different ways of seeing the world—a focus on details and minimizing uncertainty (left hemisphere) or on the whole and maximizing completeness and consistency (right hemisphere)—then the workplace won't look the same anymore.

Left-brain skills are essential in the workplace. Most work requires attention to details. We would not have progressed as societies or in business without a heavy dose of left hemisphere. Work needs to get done, and left brains are attentive to duty, organization, logic, and precision. In a pre-AI world, left-brain dominant personalities were often the ones who get the bulk of work done.

I am not anti-left hemisphere, but AI is left-brained too. We need left-brain aspects at work, but not as much as we used to. AI's appetite for such work is enormous. That trend should accelerate in the future.

If people spend too much of their time and energy on details and the achievement of certainty, or too much of their training on it, then the skills of the right brain can atrophy. The result of too little right-brain skill can have devastating effects on the workplace. It can result in deluded, inhuman, bureaucratic, and change-resistant environments.

Delusion

I spent much of my career leading groups of about fifty top-notch scientists and administrators. I found one consistent barometer of employee growth potential—whether the employee was a good self-assessor.

Those who were the star performers often agreed with criticisms. In my experience they were harder on themselves than were their reviews. The strong self-assessors advanced and grew more and more capable.

The weakest self-assessors did not. They could still be good performers in a niche, but they were slower to learn new skills or embrace new problems, and less likely to show curiosities outside their historical roles. They often did not see themselves as others saw them. The weak self-assessors were the least self-critical.

The left brain does not self-evaluate. The right brain has the centers for theory of mind (how to think about oneself or another), much of people's emotional capacity, and the ability to deal with multi-faceted challenges that have many uncertainties. The left brain tends toward black-or-white and believes what it values is all there is to be valued.

That means the left hemisphere can get delusional—even fashioning bizarre interpretations of the world. The left brain loves explaining. If the left has a lot of information, then the explanation could be fine. On the other hand, if it has highly incomplete information the explanation could be right in a narrow sense...given what it knows...but makes no sense overall. (Ahem—doesn't that sound like ChatGPT?)

If you tell the right hemisphere of a split-brain patient to stand, and then ask the left brain why they stood, the left's penchant for explaining shows clearly.[92] The left brain has no idea why they stood; it wasn't told. Yet it'll make up an explanation anyway; it won't say "I don't know." The left doesn't process meaning or consistency very well. Any old excuse will do that fits the detail it has observed. The right hemisphere doesn't have the same confusion.

If great self-evaluation is so important, how might a company measure that? (...understanding that it may be correlated to success rather than causative.)

Some companies use personality tests for hiring and team building. There are many problems in doing so.[93] Intelligent test takers can manipulate the results toward what they believe the employer will value. Often the questions require binary answers, but personalities can vary considerably depending on the context. People may be extroverts in one type of situation and introverts in another, for example. Even if those factors are minimized, these are self-reports. Many people don't see themselves as others see them.

It is indicative of this delusion that everyone I have met thinks they are a big-picture thinker. Some truly are, and the others are deluded enough to think they are. (I'm not sure in which category I fit!) As I write, there's a wry smile on my face imagining that many if not most readers are projecting negative left-brain attributes onto others while ignoring it in themselves. We all are both left- and right-brained and exhibit the pros and cons of each. Delusion is a fundamental human problem.

Delusion can manifest at the organizational level too. Organizations are collections of personalities after all, and there's some indication that left-hemisphere thinking is more common in senior leaders.[94]

Phil Rosenweig discusses such misconceptions in his book *The Halo Effect*.[95] Once a business is successful, there is a tendency to think what they are doing culturally or strategically is what led to that success. Rosenweig says it may be the other way around; strong company performance may have improved morale and culture—not leadership actions.

Among other factors, it is a confusion between correlation and causation. Perhaps fortune was involved in the success. Maybe the company had a position devoid of direct competitors or got a lucky break in its marketing efforts. The counterfactual can't be observed. Could the company have done even better with different internal decisions and processes?

Business and leadership research can add to this delusion. Case studies are a favorite in those communities. Studies often focus on the obvious success or failure cases and look for common factors, but counterexamples can be ignored. The companies with great performance and a horrible culture may not be part of the analysis.

These delusions permeate an organization. It's easy for a leader to show the bottom line or impact, or the promise of those, and use that to pat themself on the back. An overinflated view of the company can set in. I've seen people succumb...holding onto company stock way beyond market rationale or emulating poor leadership under the assumption that such a style is inherent to success. Steve Jobs was known for his interpersonal unfriendliness, for example. After his death and a best-selling biography, some seemed to copy that behavior without considering that his success didn't require it.

The left brain is wired to be gullible. It takes the adoption of a far different perspective to pull us out of those traps. Only the right brain's capabilities can do that.

Inhumanity

In 2002 psychologists Delroy Paulhus and Kevin Williams at the University of British Columbia defined the Dark Triad of subclinical (below pathogenic diagnosis) personalities: narcissism, Machiavellianism, and psychopathy.[96] A fourth, usually sadism, is sometimes added...forming the Dark Tetrad. These personality features are strongly associated with malevolent characteristics, including callousness, manipulation, lack of empathy and compassion, and less belief in others' good intentions. They are also conditions that involve left-brain dominance.

Paulhus and Williams were challenging a specific theory by many at the time that the Dark Triad conditions are all coincident. If you show one, you show them all. They found correlations between these personality features but not complete overlap. Later, when business and leadership research caught onto the term, Dark Triad personalities became poster children for poor leaders.

Narcissists are hung up on themselves. They truly feel others are inferior. Aspects of this personality include entitlement and sense of superiority, grandiosity, and dominance. They can be charismatic and attentive to appearance, so they can sometimes give a good first impression.

Machiavellianism scores high on interpersonal manipulation. They can be quite intelligent and use many approaches to get their way, including charm. They are self-interested, callous, and immoral. They will have different behaviors for different people, or in private versus in public, but those behaviors are chosen to maximize their own power. The adaptivity of their approach to people shows some right hemisphere strength, but the lack of caring for people demonstrates weakness too.

Psychopaths have low levels of empathy, like the other two conditions, but they are more impulsive and threatening. Psychopaths will tend to define people in binary terms—either with them or against them. They have little regard for other lives and are considered the most dangerous of the three in that they will take risks.

The dark triad traits appear to have significant genetic influences, though Machiavellianism seems to be more influenced by upbringing and environment than the others.[97] They are more prevalent in men.[96] Genes aren't everything though. Scientists observe that narcissism is higher in younger adults than older ones.[98]

Dark Triad personalities can create havoc in an organization. One or more of these types will be familiar to you if you've been in the workforce long enough. It is thought that they are in leadership at disproportionate levels, and they are toxic.[99] Unfortunately, those individuals may not be rooted out if the company is doing well despite such personalities, or if they've had enough time to surround themselves with those who will protect their position, either from a sense of duty or fear.

Bureaucracy

Left-brain characteristics can manifest in systemic ways as well. One of the indicators is a yearning for control.

In the movie *Meet the Parents*, there is a scene I find hysterical. Ben Stiller's character has an encounter with a flight attendant at the airport terminal. He is waiting in line to board the plane while the attendant calls out the row numbers that can board. He waits...and waits. The funny part is that there is no line; despite that, the flight attendant carries on with her routine and rules.

Rules are necessary, but they are always imperfect. They may have been created for one purpose but get stretched beyond their original intent. Their enactment may have been a reaction to one unusual overstep. I find that people often forget why a rule exists but continue to enforce it. Rules are potentially dangerous to workers when they replace contextually rich judgment.

The early development of AI demonstrates the problems with rules.[100] In roughly the 60s through 80s, the prevailing AI approach was rule-based decision systems. They were based on a series of logical rules like "if A then B, otherwise C" or similar.

Giant systems of tens of thousands of rules were created, for medical diagnosis as an example, but mostly they languished in research labs and never made it to operation. AI developers ran into lots of major challenges.

Say the AI was supposed to diagnose diabetes. There could be rules about weight, diet, test results, or other indicators of the two types of diabetes. Inevitably there are exceptions to these simple rules. Ask a doctor for a decision tree for their diagnoses and they will probably say "it depends." Ditto for many types of workers. They're telling you that context matters. For example, what if the patient has other medical conditions in addition to potential diabetes? Then additional rules will have to be created to account for those possibilities. What if they have three other conditions? Even worse. Developers of rule-based AI (often called Expert Systems) were constantly patching up holes in the logic by adding more rules. Eventually the rules would contradict one another in some way, or a minor change in data quality or patient situation could kick off a cascade of strange rule interpretations. Rule-based systems are inherently brittle.

Businesses that have lots of rules are also prone to breaking when unusual situations occur. Such environments attract dutiful personalities that are comfortable with lots of structure and top-down control. If you have too many of those people—if nobody knows why they're making your job harder because they've long ago stopped asking why it's important—then your culture likely won't be good at being malleable in other ways. Bureaucracy usually eliminates variability...making behaviors and processes more consistent. There is an inherent tension between that structure and friendliness toward people. The latter requires being willing to examine each situation uniquely and make a judgment instead of blindly following a rule.

Rules are only one manifestation of control. So, too, is enforcement of rigid processes or norms or lack of adaptability to situational conditions. For example, if a certain style of communication is enforced, then an organization and its leaders can become detuned from the personalities on the other side of the table. A more adaptive organization would pick its communication mode and style to suit the audience—not to enforce conformity. Different personalities demand adaptable approaches, yet oh so many bosses have one style for everyone. I guess I could say that for non-bosses too!

Such context inflexibility—either in norms, rules, or behaviors—reflects an excessively left-brain culture. Coupled with the delusion of perhaps undeserved success, it leads to strong change resistance.

Change Resistance

It seems schools and businesses haven't already pivoted to wisdom (or the 21st-Century Skill list) because they've created a self-licking ice cream cone driven by excessive left-brain leanings. The status quo works not only to prevent change but to lock in power bases. Change is a problem for left brains that want to minimize uncertainty.

The phrase "self-licking ice cream cone" has primarily been used in a political context. It refers to a self-perpetuating system...one that seems to exist to sustain itself. The ingredients for that dynamic are in place if too many left-brain dominant people occupy an organization or a culture. The few foxes in the mix become head scratchers—confused by the inability of their peers to see the forest for the trees but powerless to affect it.

There may be few aspects of a business that are consciously self-licking. Maybe a top executive or employee feels their own power or position becomes the main goal. Yet I suspect it is more often a subconscious drive that affects behavior. Workers may believe they are serving a grander purpose while simultaneously creating the incentives and conditions to perpetuate the status quo.

Once left-brain dominant personalities are in power, they can lead an organization into a potentially damaging positive feedback loop where the imbalance becomes progressively worse. Similar personalities are emphasized in hiring. If change agents make it through the hiring wicket, then their impotence in the face of unrelenting bureaucracy and toxic personalities hastens their exit.

I look for certain clues of left-brain, change-resistant work cultures, such as:

- Do they have continuous change processes—where change is expected, and progress is measured by the change—or do they approach change as an occasional, episodic thing?
- Is there hypocrisy? Do the company values say one thing, but boss or worker behaviors demonstrate something different?
- Is change often interpreted as doubling down—doing more of the same?
- Has the culture forgotten why it does things the way it does?
- Is strategy infused with how the organization would adapt to changes beyond its control, or is it crossing its fingers that things stay as-is?

Schooling—as an industry—seems to show several of those change resistant symptoms.

Strong right brains keep us from getting in echo chamber traps and are always looking for change. Unfortunately, its "what else is out there" orientation can mean they are less focused and organized. This can keep heavily right-brain people from attaining the power they need to enact change.

Any big change is challenging and must deal with the momentum of long-term practices, but a pivot toward wisdom will be fought every step of the way by left-brain personalities and bureaucracies who neither desire nor see the need for change.

INTUITION AND THE ASSOCIATIVE NETWORK

Let me go back to how I started the chapter, by discussing intuition and its role in wisdom. The discussion of left and right brain is a useful dichotomy that parallels many aspects of expertise and wisdom. It also shows the nonverbal nature of the right hemisphere. Much of the right brain's understanding comes unconsciously...from intuition.

What makes one person's intuition wiser than another's? Our intuition is powered by a network of concepts, ideas, and individual information pieces. They're connected in a web of associations. Whether we have strong or weak intuition is related to the richness of that associative network.

Do you ever wonder how newborn babies figure things out? They clearly don't have knowledge at birth. Memorizing state capitals comes later. They don't yet think in language. They presumably don't start with many concepts about the world and how they fit into it—other than what they could glean *in utero*.

Babies are driven by what psychologists call core affect—their body sensations and the feelings those invoke.[101] It has two pillars:

valiance (pleasant to unpleasant) and arousal (low to high stimulation). Reactions to changes in core affect—like having a bowel movement—aren't consciously considered by a baby that doesn't have the conceptual skills to process it. The reactions are intuitive.

Over time, notions like good and bad emerge from core affect. Eventually good and bad get language labels. Sensations are recognized with more nuance as situations provide feedback. Good and bad concepts generate more flavors: annoyance, excitement, love, sad, sick, worried. Those eventually get language labels too.

Many other abstract concepts do not map to words—like the way mom scrunches her face when the baby makes a certain sound. The scrunch may nevertheless be an important concept to recognize if it's connected to core affect. Eventually aspects of good and bad can be relatively disconnected from the body sensations (though not completely; the continued embodiment of thinking is a hot topic).

We start life with a few central concepts—central because they have relevance to many aspects of life. To use an analogy, they define the roots or trunk of the association tree. Central concepts (trunks) spawn more specific branches and eventually leaves.

Our intuition relies on a vast network of associated ideas, concepts, and information...all starting from notions of how our bodies feel.

We don't know a great deal about the brain's extremely complicated associative network, but its structure will follow certain principles. Research shows that associative systems that arise through natural processes, such as social, economic, disease, or ecological ones, have structural similarities.

Imagine a network of the interactions among people. People in those networks vary widely in how many other people they're connected to. The shut-in elderly person has few connections while the socialite seems to know everyone. The statistics in such networks show lots of people with few connections but a few with a ton. This distribution of connectivity is eerily similar across a wide range of phenomena.[102] The number of connections of one entity to others in an associative network is referred to as its centrality.

In the brain's associative network—as in a social network—some things are more central. They hold the network together and bridge thought realms, like the trunk and main branches of a tree do for the tiny branches and leaves. Details are mere leaves on that massive tree; we'd hardly miss them if gone. More general principles—like core affect is for a baby—are more central.

I think that's what the police and epidemiologists had in common in the game they played. They had central concepts related to connect-the-dots investigative work because they had experiences like the situation posed in the game. Such concepts are big branches of the imaginary tree. They are more central concepts, coming in handy in several contexts.

Like a tree, the leaves can't form out of thin air. Central roots and branches come first. So too with the brain's associative network. The more generally useful concepts must come first. Central concepts are thus naturally transferable ones. Transferability in learning parlance refers to usability across application domains...like the conceptual bridges between policing and public health.

Notions are transferable only if the concepts are robust. That is, they must have both accuracy and nuance. If a baby misinterprets its body signals, or whether a caretaker is improving them, then a concept that the caretaker makes them feel better will be somewhat inaccurate. Mess up that concept because a caretaker is giving inconsistent or emotionally damaging care, and a baby could have a difficult time forming concepts regarding loving attachment.

Central concepts are also important because they can spawn new subsidiary concepts. The concept of body comfort in a baby can spawn new ones related to interpersonal interaction (e.g., notions of love and happiness and how to recognize those) or body sensations (e.g., this feeling means hunger and that one is intestinal discomfort). Errors in existing concepts can create the need for other ones. If mom or dad isn't always happy when they interact with a baby, then ideas about why that may be so can augment the baby's associative network.

Central concepts tend toward the abstract. Narrow information pieces and concepts necessarily don't relate to much else unless our life circumstances force us to use the information regularly. Even then, the more abstract concept will attract connections by virtue of their generality which results in frequency of use. Brains strengthen what they use often.

Life's central concepts are at the heart of what human beings describe and debate. They are the concepts that get used across the arts, humanities, science, and business. They relate to the most often used words in language, or to core reusable principles, sometimes at a high abstraction level. They include the assumptions and rules-of-thumb that every discipline relies upon.

Wisdom's intuition cares most about central concepts, whereas the less intuitive left hemisphere hangs out nearer to the leaves. The right pushes the brain toward connecting more central abstract concepts, while the left drills down toward the less-connected details.

Professor Tetlock's superforecasters—the jack-of-all-trades— must have many transferable concepts, as illustrated in Figure 2.

The hedgehog knows some things with depth, but there are only a few of those things. Maybe a worker knows physics, math, and computer science deeply, for example, corresponding to the three clusters in the hedgehog network shown in Figure 2. The connections between the discipline clusters would tend to be more direct than for a fox. A hedgehog may not have the exposure to far-flung disciplines to form linkages with more general concepts. For example, a certain type of physics challenge might need to use math and computer concepts, but in a hedgehog that association might be without the context of how those same methods are useful in other fields. Still, I included one transferable concept (dark circle) in the hedgehog network that would theoretically recognize the utility of the methodological connection.

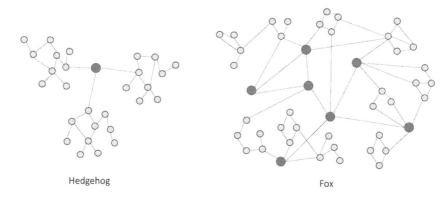

Hedgehog

Fox

Figure 2. Illustrative comparison of the associative networks of an expert "hedgehog" and a wise "fox." Transferable concepts are the dark gray circles.

The foxes' network covers more ground in a whole-world sense, as there are more topics represented (more clusters). However, each topic is understood with less depth than the hedgehog's domain knowledge (fewer nodes in each cluster). What the foxes have that the hedgehogs don't is more abstract concepts that connect disciplines, as shown by the gray nodes. Those are the transferable concepts. They could be about a process for doing or deciding, a heuristic, or a philosophy. They are the meaning-laden glue to associative network storytelling.

Central, transferable concepts are the hooks onto which new information can connect. If we are trying to learn something that has no relationship with our associative network...like in memorizing detail...then artificial associations must be created. That's why memory palaces and other mnemonics are used.

Wisdom relies upon the right brain, and specifically on central, transferable concepts in our brain's intuitive associative network.

§

One of the enigmas of wisdom is that it seems amorphous and inexplicable compared to the concreteness of expertise. That's because its base of operation in the brain is in the nonverbal right hemisphere and in unconscious, intuitive processing.

Modern society, with its left-brain dominance, can be dismissive of wisdom. That's a mistake. There is great evidence that intuitive, right-brain processing is critically important. Conscious deliberation is unusual in large part because it is slower and more energy consuming. Even when we think we are consciously deciding, research shows that is often an illusion, with the decision being reported to consciousness but determined without awareness.[103]

The intangible and unconscious attributes of wisdom create tremendous challenges for explicit teaching. It will be hard for many to accept the pivot I'm advocating without the identification of the concepts which need learning. In educator terminology, the learning scaffold is unclear. It's also individually variable, making consistent prerequisites hard to define.

If one were to design a series of lectures to impart aspects of wisdom to students, it would be both ineffective and incomplete. Incomplete because so much of wisdom uses nonverbal concepts, and ineffective because right-brain intuition doesn't learn well from lecture.

Instead, wisdom is learned by experience and associated reflection—especially varied experiences that engender big-picture lessons. That's the subject of the next chapter.

5.

EXPERIENCE

*Good judgment comes from experience, and experience
comes from bad judgment.*

Rita Mae Brown[104]

I was working on a disaster management project many years ago when one of our advisors introduced me to war gaming. Ask any war gaming expert and they will regale you with its long and storied history, stretching back centuries, and adopted by most militaries.[105] Modern war games aim to prepare leaders for strategic decision making involving somewhat unpredictable adversaries. Crucial cognitive skills for military leaders are to adapt to a new situation, improvise to achieve goals, and to balance multiple objectives that change in importance. War games allow the practice of those skills in a more efficient way than field exercises and with the incremental unfurling of a situation like in real life.

"No war plan survives the first shot," goes the military adage that acknowledges the uncontrollability of war. Carl von Clausewitz—a Prussian general in the early 1800s—is best known as a military theorist. He defined three characteristics of war that affect human decision making: fog, friction, and chance.[106] Fog refers to uncertainty, including the inability to know everything about the adversary or your own forces. Friction is a trickier concept. It refers to practical constraints to knowing or getting things done. One part of the military could know something, for example, that another doesn't but should. Chance is self-explanatory. It's the combination of fog, friction, and chance that puts onus on military leaders—really on all leaders—to be capable of wise improvisation.

Adaptability isn't tested by retrospective case studies where the outcome is already known—nor by infrequent and expensive field exercises that are more about orchestration of the pieces. War games put military leaders in time-evolving situations, throw in monkey wrenches, and have them decide.

The topic of war gaming came up during the disaster management project because first responders don't get that kind of training. Our military has some of the best abstract and conceptual thinkers in the world...especially regarding leadership. It's no accident. The military spends tremendous energy preparing them in classroom and field settings. They also rotate them through various jobs as they ascend the hierarchy to arm them with a range of perspectives.

In contrast, homeland disaster management is almost entirely learn-as-you-go. Leaders are dropped into the deep water. They don't have the budget and spare personnel to do frequent training and still get their jobs done. When they do participate in preparedness exercises, those drills are often scripted ahead of time, including the decisions.

The advisor conducted an informal war game with us as a demonstration of that tool. Our team of game players led an imaginary infantry force expected to imminently engage an adversary. We had to decide how to maneuver our force and defeat the enemy. Force preservation and territory gain were dual goals. The team collaborated to study what our personnel and weapons could do compared to the adversary arsenal. We examined various tactical approaches.

We agreed on a plan and played the game using feedback from the instructor.

We got some surprising information soon after deploying our forces. A previously unnoticed adversary force appeared over the crest of a hill and flanked our force. Moreover, our home base was emptied out and the enemy had a clear path to it. The rest was no contest. Our force got crushed. We were victims of fog.

The instructor expected us to make that mistake. It was the point of the exercise. We'd commit all our forces, and when something unexpected happened, we wouldn't be in the right position to respond.

He was teaching us to hedge our bet by holding back forces in the face of uncertainty so we could still respond to monkey wrenches. He was teaching an aspect of improvisation—to expect the unexpected. The power of that fictional game hammered home the lesson in a way that the "always leave forces in reserve for unexpected contingencies" bullet point never would have.

It was even better to fail than succeed in the game. An advantage of gaming is that the students can fail, learn the lesson, and do it better the next time. Failure has a way of begging for explanation that self-assured success won't demand. Doing something that caused failure—even if in this imaginary battle—conveyed emotional power that dwarfed reading about it. Doing something...not just thinking about doing...made the mental struggles, distractions, and stresses more salient.

A game experience isn't like a real one of course, but in some ways it might be better. A real battle could have made it harder to learn the lesson than this carved out situation. In war, other people's decisions would interact with ours. There might be more than stress; it could be fear. That could change observational power. So could fatigue. A real battle might be lengthy, and brains do a worse job learning from situations that evolve more slowly. The hedging lesson could be lost in the mix—especially if the battle succeeded. If it didn't, the failure would be tragic as well as instructive...with emotion possibly obscuring reason.

Still, I couldn't buy into hedging as a universal principle in the face of situational uncertainty. If it's clear that my force would be overwhelmed no matter what, then retreating to safety and not fighting is a better bet. General Washington used retreat a few times in the Revolutionary War, and it made all the difference. Unless the battle is so critical that I have no choice. Holding back forces when already the underdog doesn't seem sensible. If there is any shot at all it's because we get as equivalent as possible to the other force or exercise our own forms of tactical surprise. That might require going all-in.

The game was an experience that made the hedging concept tangible, but for it to be a robust concept, the limits of it had to be tested...if only mentally. The game primed reflection about other contexts or analogous dilemmas. George sneaking the army back across the East River from Long Island in dense fog was a counterexample to the game. Hedging depended on having sufficient resources to even consider a battle and enough to hold something back and still be confident in any success.

I also didn't see how readily the lesson applied to the disaster management community, though the instructor's main goal was to demonstrate a game construct instead of conveying a specific lesson. Holding back resources when people are in crisis gets people hurt and decision makers fired. There are other factors that matter in the homeland.

I started thinking of hedging as risk management more so than a way to mitigate uncertainty. That notion poked in from the concept of financial diversification. The broader one invests the more confidence there is that a catastrophic outcome will be avoided. Yet that assumes safety is the chief criterion. Those who win at poker or wealth accumulation at some point take a big risk where there is the biggest potential payout. Maybe it's best to hedge when minimizing a worst-case outcome and go all-in when complete failure is allowable to maximize the return.

Hedging can connect to other abstract principles. Deciding whether to hedge or not...if done wisely...must consider many other situational factors. What is the risk tolerance of the situation? Can complete failure be tolerated? A rich person might take the chance on a more lucrative payoff by going all-in on one financial investment, whereas a poorer person will need to keep the risk of losing it all relatively low and hedge via investment diversification.

The hedging concept becomes more robust and useful with more examples. The tradeoff between payoff and safety is only one consideration. Along the way the concept becomes connected to more situations than the infantry battle scenario. The branch in our associative network gets thicker, connecting to more and more leaf clusters, and to other big branches. Perhaps it connects to the notion that tradeoffs are common features of complex systems (e.g., "you can't have your cake and eat it, too," "there's no free lunch"). The concept becomes more central in the brain's associative network as more situations and analogies are considered. The combination of experience, variation, and musing can create stories that enhance the transferability of the hedging concept.

In the last chapter I described the underpinnings of wisdom. This chapter is about how wisdom is learned through experience and reflection.

EXPERIENCE FEEDS INTUITION

It took the devastating stretch from December 2004 to October 2005 to shock my colleagues and me into getting off the sidelines. The Indian Ocean Tsunami (230,000 deaths), Hurricane Katrina (1,800 deaths), and the Kashmir Earthquake (100,000 deaths), were unparalleled in collective memory. My colleagues and I decided to try to help disaster response, especially for large-scale events.

There were several obvious problems.

Disaster response seemed a pickup game, but I wondered how much of the chaos and uncertainty was avoidable. Nobody seemed to have a playbook for decision making beyond a structure for organizing responsibilities—despite the clear knowledge that each region was primed for a disaster of that type. It was a far cry from the planning efforts in the U.S. military to which I was accustomed.

Information needed for decision making is dangerously scarce when a large disaster strikes. Awareness of the situation could shrink quickly—or never form well to begin with. Lots of volunteers or other jurisdictions donate situation surveillance, analysis, and response forces, but they are not used to working together. There's often no easy way to share the resulting information. Well-meaning but uninvited "disaster tourists" who bring along their favorite technology or resources can add more distraction than impact. If they do get the information, responders may not have the experience to interpret or trust in a source they've never used before. Some of the individuals will have never managed a large-scale disaster.

Then there is coordination. In the U.S. and many other countries there is a command and coordination structure for incidents of all sizes. In the U.S. it's the Incident Command System (ICS). It defines roles and responsibilities and how to evolve that structure as the situation grows. In contrast, there may be little consistent structure for an international incident (depending on the disaster locale). The ability to coordinate in real-time can vary widely.

CAL Fire was a logical organization to work with in our initial forays. They are California's firefighting lead—an increasingly difficult and dangerous role as nature and housing intersect. We began working with them because they are self-aware and forward-thinking. ICS was modeled on the system CAL Fire invented decades ago.

They also deal with big fires every year plus the occasional earthquake or flood. We didn't have to guess where a disaster would land. It would happen somewhere in California soon. That's bad for California, but it's good for technologists who need ways to test, iterate, and improve their constructions.

I expected to hear about technology deficiencies when I first met CAL Fire leadership. We were there as designated geeks after all.

They did talk about those problems. Their response forces got spread broadly—often in communication dead zones. They were forced to relay basics like current position over a radio party-line instead of using the limited bandwidth on tactics, strategy, and emergencies within the disaster. Plans were updated by in-person coordination with a map spread across the hood of a vehicle. The fire could move tens of miles between command meetings. They gave us plenty of ideas for new technology. MIT Lincoln Lab built a prototype system to improve situational awareness and coordination. There were many iterations with co-developer CAL Fire until they were ready to take over.[107] Its use spread to other parts of the world.[108]

My surprise was that technology wasn't their biggest concern. They were worried the senior leaders were retiring, and there was a couple-decade age gap to the next round of leaders. They had high confidence in those people but wondered whether they had enough experience. They understood how critical experience is in building the intuitions demanded for large fire management.

Psychologist Gary Klein learned the importance of firefighter experience decades ago.[109] His research on decision making is matched by few other luminaries. His analysis showed that firefight leaders usually don't think about alternative options at all; they sense the situation, unconsciously match it to a prototype of a similar one, and jump to an action based on that experience. One experienced firefighter described a house fire to Klein. He had ordered an evacuation less than a minute before the floor above the basement collapsed. The decision was based on what the fire chief called a sixth sense. Clues were present to suggest a basement fire they couldn't see: ineffective watering on the first floor and heat on the first floor without much noise. The chief didn't consciously think about those factors. He decided entirely with intuition.[109]

I noticed the emphasis on intuition in my interactions with CAL Fire. The first thing the Incident Commander of a large fire would do was go to the fire. That was often a long way from the command location...these fires can be big...and I questioned why physical presence was necessary. Maybe it was a way to coordinate with other command levels face-to-face, or perhaps to fill a yearning for being part of the action, like in their younger days?

After a while I realized those weren't the reasons...or not the dominant ones. They needed to see the fire. They could develop a sense about what kind of beast it is. They unconsciously noted the way it grabbed oxygen, the type and amount of fuel in its path, the wind and terrain patterns, and the smell and heat. In-person experience gave them intuition on how to tackle a blaze. They felt the right answer.

That we rely on intuition is...well...intuitive to most people. We don't have to be decision-making gurus to know that experience matters in our performance. Less obvious is that our decisions are usually unconscious. If we are to improve the intuition that's so important for wisdom, then it's important to dig into how experience affects it, and what kinds of experience are better or worse for a high-performing gut feel.

What is the linkage between experience and the intuition that wisdom needs?

INTUITIVE DECISION MAKING

The scientific method prescribes controlling as many variables as possible to generate results that can best answer a specific hypothesis. The more that's uncontrollable, the more difficult it becomes to generate specific insights. Experiments of physical phenomena are easiest to control. Those experiments usually allow creation of an environment in a laboratory that isn't different from outside it. The aspect of the world under study doesn't change by walking in the lab door.

Experimental controllability becomes much more difficult when studying complex systems—especially life forms. Even studying a single cell has experimental reproducibility and natural world relevance issues. The exact state of the cells can't be completely known, and the environment given the cells is never the same in a lab as it is in natural circumstances. Those issues become even bigger when analyzing human beings.

At the time Klein did his firefighting research, conventional models of decision making were often so-called rational ones, where a range of options are explicitly considered, each are evaluated according to various criteria, and they are prioritized in some way to choose the best. Lab-based experiments on decision making showed a rational process does improve decision performance, but under various conditions decision makers would naturally adopt a more intuitive approach.[110] The explicit decision processes often exercised in a work setting—where a ton of options are ideated, scored against some criteria, and ranked based on those scores—can be useful approaches. However, many people will have already decided unconsciously.

Experimental design that tries to reduce uncertainties in the lab has the danger that the results might not be relevant outside the lab. Real-world conditions are often sacrificed in many lab experiments on decision making, and those tend to reduce the impact of intuition and experience. There might not be time pressure, allowing people to take a more deliberative process. Decision challenges are often about something the participants haven't experienced. There is little opportunity under those conditions to trigger the associative network that's intuition's foundation.

A discussion I had with an experienced trauma surgeon years ago illustrates the paralyzing effect a lack of experience can have on decision making in real life. She explained how new doctors with plenty of knowledge—but little experience—can be deer-in-the-headlights in real situations. If a patient comes in with a gunshot wound, the rookie docs often want to get test results before they operate that might indicate internal damage. That information comes at a cost. Patients might bleed out while waiting for test results. An experienced surgeon would understand when the risk of delay was too great compared to the information value from extra tests. Experience teaches trauma surgeons to sometimes accept an educated guess over certainty.

If you're good at something, then much of the skill will be intuitive (a term implying big-picture, right-brain insights) or automatic (with a left-brain connotation). Skilled musicians aren't thinking consciously about finger movements, breath control, or technique.

Conscious control of fingers on a keyboard can't be done at the speed and precision that's required. It becomes coordinated and effortless when it is baked into the subconscious. Ditto for any cognitive skill.

Quick decision making is a human necessity.[111] Conscious deliberation is energy consuming and slow. Given the number of decisions we need to make—including every hand movement in a piano piece—deliberating on everything would paralyze us. We reserve it for novel situations. The inexperienced are put into more novel conditions

Gary Klein was saying that the firefighters—and decision makers in many other communities he has studied since—don't behave in real life like they do in contrived laboratory situations. He posited that in natural settings, those who are experienced mentally leap to an answer.[112] They use intuition.

Lab studies of chess decision making do illuminate the importance of intuition because experience is allowed, and a ranking scale is available to signify ability. It turns out chess experts don't consider more moves than novices, but their move options are better.[113] The chess masters are great at quickly recognizing the board and game situation. They get that way by analyzing many games...especially those of other experts. They make great decisions quickly because they immediately recognize the board as a whole and jump to the small set of moves that are worth trying. Consciousness can then focus on a small move set nominated by intuition rather than an exhaustive set generated more consciously.

Klein described a new model of human decision making, shown at a high level in Figure 3.[114] The outer loop is the more common decision pathway. People unconsciously recognize patterns in situations and follow a corresponding action the brain has associated with that pattern. Often it is the first option considered. Klein believes the unconscious doesn't consider many options either.[115] That doesn't jive with our sense for needing to make the best decision, but in much of life fast and pretty good beats slow and optimal.

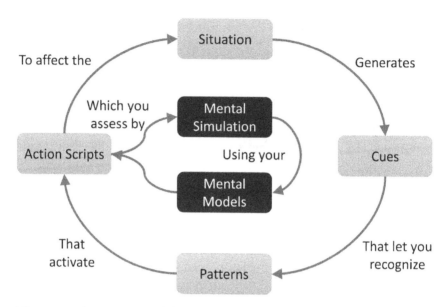

Figure 3. Summary of the Recognition-Primed Decision Model

If the situation isn't like the cues from our experience, then the loop in the middle of Figure 3 can be used to consider what-ifs. That process can be conscious and slow, but often it is also unconscious and fast.

If this is how we are wired to make decisions, then what skills would a great intuitive decision maker have versus a poor one? Great intuition will be able to perceive aspects of a situation that matter, some of which could be subtle. It will be able to recognize combinations of situational aspects that are a meaningful pattern. Superb intuition will be able to understand if the pattern is typical or unusual and have a rich ability to mentally model what might happen because of various choices.

If all that sounds really abstract, then join the club. Nobody precisely knows what the brain is intuiting. Intuitions are often based on tacit knowledge that by definition is difficult to express. That makes it difficult to transfer it to others by telling them. Brains need to absorb it via the residue of experience.

If you're confused about how left and right hemisphere talents relate to intuition, then it's probably because you're considering them to be coupled when they are largely independent features. The left brain does pattern-matching and jumps to answers, too, but it does so on detailed and precise information like with the chess example. We are more likely to refer to left-side, unconscious processing as instinct or habit. The right brain is chewing on more uncertainty and a broader view of a situation. Both sides process a lot unconsciously, but the right side's form is more commonly called intuition.

Intuition isn't necessarily correct; it can be bad or good at its job. It's a thinking short cut, and some short cuts don't work out well. However, it's not an inherently bad and unreliable creature that we're supposed to overcome with logic and concentration. It's the complement to those qualities. It's how we exhibit experience in our skills. Ignore experiential learning and decisions will be worse. Rely on intuition at the exclusion of deliberation, and we aren't learning to question our guts. Decisions will be worse that way too.

VARIATION

I want to distinguish something that is intuitive from something that is automatic. Solving the Rubik's Cube in my childhood involved two coupled aspects. One was mentally manipulating a set of moves as if it were one; the same sequences would be used time and again. After much practice, those sequences were automatic and unvarying. However, deciding which move sequence should be taken based on the layout of the cube was different. That was never the same since the cube's current state was always different. That aspect benefitted from intuition.

Automaticity needs repetition, but intuition needs variation. It is in making some sort of generalization—finding a commonality between things—that concepts are formed. That's true whether teaching AI a concept or teaching one to a person. It's a fundamental.

One of the most common uses of AI (and our noggins) is categorization that seeks to label a set of information as belonging to two or more buckets. The categories can be true or false, for example, if asking whether a portion of a medical image is potentially concerning or whether an image contains my face. It could be a long list of buckets if the image analysis is being asked to label the objects in a scene or indicate what type of disease the medical image shows. Categorization decisions are everywhere: buy or sell; hard rock, country, or R&B; fraud or legit; lend money or not.

Categorizations require AI to find one or more decision boundaries. On one side of the boundary are examples that fit one category, and on the other side the examples fit a different bucket. For an AI that tries to identify images containing my face, one side of the boundary would be the range of possible images that include my face, and the other side would be those that do not. In real life there aren't an infinite number of images of my face (thank goodness for that!), so AI (or our brains) must estimate the best boundary it can with the limited examples it is given.

AI is completely naïve until told not to be. One of the key tasks in AI development is making sure the examples used to train the AI are a good representation of the range intended in its eventual use. A single example doesn't cut it. Give AI the same picture of my face repeatedly, and it should be expected to be horrible at recognizing other pictures of me. It will do much better if it is given a wide range of Tim face images. Yes...unfortunately including the images with silly expressions, the ones from bad angles with double chins, some with and without facial hair, and the one with the giant Elton John-like sunglasses. It's precisely the images that are most unusual that are important for defining the edges of the Tim-face category.

A ton of Tim images isn't sufficient though. There also must be a diverse set of images that don't include my mug. If it's given only Tim faces in training, then it will think every face it sees afterward is also Tim. There's essentially no categorization decision to make if examples aren't provided on both sides of the decision boundary.

I was thinking about this recently in the context of biomedical knowledge networks.[116] Monstrous associative networks of biological and medical information have been developed, and those are now being mined for leads on new drug targets...among other uses. The networks include associations based on evidence from technical articles, clinical trials, and curated databases of chemicals, genes, or medical conditions. A challenge to AI mining of these knowledge networks is that experiments that fail aren't often publicly documented. Ideally the network would have more than evidence of associations; it would also have evidence of the lack of some associations—which is different than being uncertain about one.

Life doesn't always provide people good examples on both sides of the decision boundary or over the full range of possibilities. Maybe romantic relationships have always failed for you because you tend to pick a similar personality type each time. You don't have a counter-example. School may have kids run math problems or science experiments that work but may not show them the ones that fail. Work may insist that taking some project risk is desired because they want creativity, but failure seems to be a career killer, so projects are scoped so they don't fail.

We have an advantage over AI of course in that we can vicariously learn about the other side of decision boundaries from other people. Reading and communicating with one another is crucial. We can hear about other people's lessons. Still, our own failures are most poignant—driving reflection that can lead to insight.

Not all experience is equal. Doing the same job your entire life can make you great at that job, but it doesn't necessarily make you able to adapt to anything else. Wisdom requires concepts that develop through experiential variation, especially experiences with big-picture lessons that the right brain can chew on. The wider the experience base, the more likely the associative network behind intuition will have something relevant to offer—if only by analogy.

Variation is a fundamental aspect of forming strong concepts undergirding intuition...whether for AI or for us.

OUR EXPERIENCE-DEPRIVED

We each have different associative networks since our experiences are different, and we have varied brain wiring. The impact of a sparser network with fewer concepts and connections between them is especially striking for socioeconomically disadvantaged children.

In 1995, Betty Hart and Todd Riley published *Meaningful Differences in the Everyday Experience of Young American Children*, and it shook the education world.[117] Betty and Todd had experience trying to improve language learning in young children, but as with other early intervention programs, the enhancements from their efforts were temporary.[118] When they measured the vocabulary of students in kindergarten, the improvements they saw in preschool from their interventions had disappeared.

They decided they needed to understand more about what was happening at home. Hart and Riley recorded an hour of natural conversation per month over two-and-a-half years in the homes of forty-two families with children between the age of ten months and three years old.

They noticed children from low-income households got far less exposure to spoken language in general and heard from a smaller vocabulary. They did a follow-up study when the children were in elementary school. The vocabulary differences at age three strongly correlated with language test scores at age nine and ten. This study has been repeated in different forms and populations in difficult-to-compare experimental setups, but most educational researchers accept the general finding that differences in early childhood exposure to language has a lasting effect.[119]

Think of this in terms of the brain's associative network. Words are labeled concepts. They're not the only concepts in the network. Most are abstract mappings between abstract things that help our minds do unconscious stuff. However, words and their associations have a special place because of their role in creating meaning around what we observe.

A lower vocabulary means fewer concepts and a weaker network for expressing oneself. Exponentially more word associations are possible in bigger networks. If there are two words, the number of associations between them is at most one. If there are a hundred words, then there can be 4,950 associations. For a thousand words or concepts there could be nearly 500,000 connections. Pretty quickly the number of possible associations gets to crazily high values. More vocabulary offers more opportunity for associations. There is much less that can be done with a sparse vocabulary than an extensive one.

Even worse than having fewer uses, a sparse language set also makes it harder to learn new language or concepts. Retention requires associating the new information with something already learned. The more we know, the easier it is to learn.

That means getting behind early in life should magnify over time. Indeed, many studies show children from low socioeconomic statuses (low-SES, which includes much more than wealth) not only have worse average cognitive ability at every age, but they also get further behind as the years progress. Children from low-SES families are an average of five years behind high-income students in literacy skills when entering high school and drop out about five times as often.[120] Those figures are shocking.

The state of the associative network is far from the only impediment to learning in low-SES populations. Ever-present worry in those populations can cut into the working memory capacity at the heart of conscious decision making.[121] Low-SES children can also exhibit more behavior problems that can affect learning.[122]

AI development shows the effect of bigger associative networks. Most machine learning uses building blocks that are crude analogs to neurons. Artificial Neural Networks (ANNs) are combinations of these neuron-like components. As mentioned in Chapter 1, there has long been hope that by making the networks bigger, more sophisticated behavior would arise from AI. It has. For example, a new version of ChatGPT was recently released that is built on GPT-4 that's a larger ANN trained on more data than the prior language model. The size of the resulting AI network is often a principal difference. The bigger network improves ChatGPT performance across a wide range of measures.[123] Across many domains, the construction of large networks is the assumed precursor to better performing AI.

Bigger networks are better performing whether in humans or for AI. However, language weaknesses in low-SES students may only be symptomatic of an associative network that has problems well beyond word count. One issue that is often neglected is the key role of episodic memory—long-term memory of previous experiences and their context. Episodic memory is key to remembering life! It's the basis of our life stories.

I think episodic memory also provides part of the structure for curiosity, learning, and retention. The Wagner Group (NOT the mercenaries Russia is using in the war with Ukraine) surveyed American adults who had taken an educational trip between ages 12 and 18.[124] Regardless of socioeconomic class, 80% of the respondents said the travel gave them more interest in what they were being taught, and about half said it affected their career choice. Those who traveled were 24% more likely to get a college degree, and the more trips the greater the effect. Two-thirds of those traveling five or more times as pre-college teens ended up graduating from college. More than half said travel helped them achieve better grades. They weren't necessarily world explorers; the criterion was an overnight trip more than fifty miles from home.

Unfortunately, less advantaged students have fewer of those opportunities. Resources for field trips are lower, and low-income parents can't afford as many summer experiences for their kids as wealthier homes. Inherently experiential domains like art, dance, or athletics can be cost-cutting or standardized test casualties. A "buckle down" mentality applied to such schools may only worsen disparities since it could deprive them of experiential-learning fuel.

One of the most devastating aspects of a disadvantaged childhood is the relative dearth of experience. Growing wisdom requires varied experience, including ones that might not be academically related.

§

If there is a commonality in how cultures throughout history regard wisdom, it's that it is a property associated with the aged. Age doesn't guarantee wisdom, but experience matters an enormous amount when making decisions.

However, for the past few decades aging workers are having trouble. People tend to think of a career as having a period of advancement, eventual plateauing, and then retirement. That's not the trend anymore. A more typical progression includes a drop in income and status beginning in your 50s followed by a retirement date set more by the employer than by the employee.

Being pushed out of a stable job in your 50s is more normal than not. One study of workers who had been in a job for five or more years entering their 50s—about half of workers that age—showed that 56% of them were eventually pushed out by their employers before the worker's desired retirement.[125] Only 10% of those shown the exit ever earned as much as they did before they were let go. The average income drop was around 40%.

This trend is worsening. The fraction of those over 50 who have been subject to financially damaging job loss has increased from 10% in 1998 to 30% in 2016.[125] The statistics are similar by location, level of education, income, or industry. The quaint notion of choosing when you want to retire is gone for most workers. As of 2014, most are forced to retire.[125]

About half of the older workers who are pushed out of their stable jobs are laid off. The other half end up leaving because of deteriorating work conditions (27%) or unexpected (a.k.a. forced) retirement (23%).[125] Of all workers who enter their 50s in stable jobs, around half of them will be forced into lower-pay work, and something in the range of 15% will encounter poor working conditions along the way. Millions of older workers are being treated poorly.

I know that among the workers with career downturns after fifty are some who haven't kept up with evolving job requirements. Their skills have atrophied. Others may produce as much but are more expensive than a younger worker.

Yet I think there is more to this than workers being out-of-touch. We seem to have lost the notion that older workers have skills that younger ones don't. Older workers are treated like squeezed lemons, with little left but the rind.

Albert-László Barabasi is a professor at Northeastern University and a lecturer at Harvard Medical School. He has now worked in academia for thirty years, but about a decade ago he began asking himself a critical question—"How long can I keep doing this?" He was listening to the lore that monumental scientific discoveries are made by people at early ages. Einstein said around thirty was the magic age where impact began to drop.

Barabasi looked at the data.[126] It showed the probability was less than 1% that he would publish a paper thirty years into his career that would be more impactful than early on. This seemingly backed up the notion that creativity is lost with age, but he dug deeper. When he factored in how many papers were published, he found that older researchers had just as good a chance of a publication having a big impact as at any other age; they just didn't produce as many papers. Their tangible productivity had changed—not their creativity.

Is that because they didn't work as hard as younger workers? Perhaps to some degree. Home responsibilities can become different, for example, as one ages. However, I have interacted with lots of professors; you won't find many at any age who are slackers. More likely they have more responsibility for coordinating, administering, or advising than younger professors do.

"This era is different," you may say. "Look at all of the young leaders in high tech." Sure...but the legend isn't necessarily the reality. Young people are far more likely to be entrepreneurs, but the older you are, the more likely your venture will lead to being listed on the stock market or being sold successfully. Professor Barabasi showed those in their 50s are twice as likely to create a successful company as those in their 30s.[126] They just don't try as often.

I think the real problem is that wisdom skills aren't properly respected. Those roles that exercise wisdom most, such as mentoring, managing, leading, and strategizing, aren't very measurable. People can believe that anyone can do it. They can't. Experience matters a great deal.

If we want to improve wisdom, we should focus on providing varied experiences—especially ones with big-picture lessons. However, there are three big problems in doing so. Real life evolves slowly—experience takes a long time. It's hard to be in the right place at the right time—experience needs opportunity. Life can only follow one timeline, missing insight from counterfactuals—experience is inherently limited. We can read about others' experiences, but it's not as useful as being forced to decide in the uncertainty of an evolving situation.

Fortunately, there is a game-changer that mitigates these experiential-learning conundrums—games.

6.

THE GAME CHANGER

Play is our brain's favorite way of learning.

Diane Ackerman[127]

Adults are accustomed to being educated through lectures...whether in school or business settings. Lectures have been the staple delivery mechanism for detailed knowledge. The problem is delivering knowledge isn't the same as understanding the concepts related to that knowledge. Teachers know that weakness but knowing it and being able to do something about it are two different things. Professor John Belcher felt his students weren't understanding deeply enough, so he sought a better way.

It was the early 2000s, and John and his leadership were concerned. The required freshman college physics class he taught was failing 10–15% of students every year. "Ever since I came, we had a high failure rate in physics," he said. "And the other required courses in chemistry, two terms of math, biology—they were typically failing 5%. We would fail twice as many."

He taught electromagnetism—the study of electric and magnetic fields and their interactions. It's a hard course for many students. John thinks that's because it's an entirely abstract subject. Electric and magnetic fields are largely invisible to every human sense. "Plus, almost no one has any intuition about electromagnetism," John said. "The kids coming here in the 1950s built ham radios with vacuum tubes, so there was a lot more understanding of electronics and electromagnetism back then. But kids in 2019 have never seen a vacuum tube." Though vacuum tubes are not relevant anymore, electricity and magnetism still are, of course, especially in the semiconductor industry. They are two of the fundamental forces of the universe.

From my own experience, electromagnetics was an especially hard conceptual subject. I remember the final exam from my college class asked me to derive Maxwell's equations, after the 19th-century English scientist. Maxwell's equations are the cornerstone of electromagnetics, but my professor never taught us how to come up with them. Somehow...after enduring my freak out moment...I figured it out. I remember because I was proud that I solved it.

Today I remember nothing of how to prove Maxwell's equations. I got lucky and figured out the derivation puzzle, but that skill offered little help understanding what the equations meant...never mind how they could manifest in the real world. Deriving the equations is a separate skill from understanding them.

Using the equations to solve problems can also be done without strong conceptual understanding. "Students can often pattern match to get past the analytic questions," Professor Belcher said. "They remember a problem that was sort of like this, and they will start writing down stuff from that memory, even though that problem is not germane to the current one. And sometimes that gets them a lot of partial credit." Solving a problem doesn't mean they understand the concepts. That understanding can be the difference between an "A" and an "F."

His students weren't average students. John is at MIT, where admitted students have an average high school GPA of 4.17, and an insane average of 1535 out of 1600 on the SAT.[128] Their students were from the top few percent of college applicants. Most of them had probably never failed anything in their academic lives; some of them may never have gotten a "B." "They're really hard on themselves," Belcher said. "They're constantly comparing themselves to other students, and there are stellar students here that are unrealistic comparisons. Failing anything was a major psychological blow to them."

Professor Belcher taught large classes with hundreds of students, and he primarily gave lectures. Lecturing is still the main teaching method for STEM (Science, Technology, Engineering, and Math) classes at U.S. and Canadian colleges.[129]

Perhaps John was a lousy lecturer? "Nah...I was a respected lecturer," he told me. "But in a typical physics lecture, you come in, and you throw stuff at 'em at a rate which they can't absorb. If you start asking the students conceptual questions, usually they won't be able to answer. That's when you really start to understand that they didn't listen to you. In a class like this—with 400 students—the lecturer doesn't get any feedback. Look...I have a Ph.D. in physics. I've seen it forever. I'm talking to a freshman who hasn't seen it forever, and sometimes I cannot intuit what they don't know.

"A great example is in teaching Faraday's Law, which is hard to understand," John explains. Faraday's law describes how magnetic fields can cause electrical currents and vice versa. It's the key principle behind electrical transformers. "When I was lecturing, I would say it's the time rate of change of the open surface integral of the magnetic field. That is so abstract." (I don't expect you readers to understand that explanation either.)

Professor Belcher got a unique opportunity. Two benefactors gave a lot of money to MIT to improve instruction, and it was open to any faculty member. "And that kind of money never comes along." He teamed with education researcher Yehudit "Judy" Dori to reform his course.

"We went to North Carolina State where they were teaching in a very hands-on way, and I was observing one group of students [explore Faraday's Law]. There's an experiment where you have a wire that's carrying current, and you put a magnet underneath it with one pole of the magnet facing toward the wire. You ask the students which way the wire is going to move before they experiment. I listened to the students argue for ten minutes about whether the wire will go down or go up. But this is a weird force that pushes the wire sideways, not up or down. People were stunned in the 18th century when they saw this kind of force. These freshmen were replicating that confusion which I didn't anticipate well in my lecturing because I've been studying this for so long."

Judy and John decided to revamp his course to an active, team-oriented learning style they felt would better get across the key concepts. Conceptual understanding, socialization, and feedback to the teacher were the priorities in the resulting TEAL (Technology-Enabled Active Learning) paradigm.[130] That model was based on the one demonstrated at North Carolina State by Robert Beichner.[131]

"We have two-hour classes, and the typical class has several stages," John explained. "There will be a short lecture on the topic, then some multiple-choice questions to test understanding. Then the professor gives an example, followed by the students working through an example at the whiteboard. Finally, the students experiment right there in the classroom."

"With the new paradigm, I still explain the theory, but [when learning about Faraday's Law] they also play hands-on with changing the magnetic flux through a wire coil." Students were also provided computer programs that helped them visualize the invisible electric and magnetic fields.

The failure rate dropped from 12% to 5% or less. Judy and John also quantified the change in student understanding from the lecture format to the TEAL format.[132] A control group taught using the conventional lecture format went from 40% conceptual understanding pre-course to about 55% afterward. The improvement doubled to around 70% post-course understanding when teaching using the TEAL format.

Though two decades ago, the TEAL paradigm is still representative of state-of-the-art teaching. It focuses on the concepts. Socialization provides varied perspectives and checks on understanding. Computers and hands-on experiments help translate the abstract notions to concrete aspects that our senses can absorb. The teacher gets frequent feedback on student understanding so they can adapt if needed.

Much of the education world has been striving for the kind of learning model that Professor Belcher adopted, but it's still unusual. "It's a lot of work to make this shift," John said. "I always say the easiest thing to do is to lecture. You're an expert in the subject area, and you can get up and show that you're an expert. You don't have to think about whether it's getting across or not."

Prior chapters set up the problem and described the principles of wisdom and how it learns. The remainder of the book is about solutions.

I have hinted at the power of gaming. In this chapter I describe why games can be the chief pillar for learning wisdom skills.

Games borrow from paradigms like TEAL in that they have people *do* instead of just *listen*, and they include socialization and frequent feedback. However, I am less interested in games for teaching narrow concepts that are relevant to expertise (e.g., Faraday's Law). The games I care about try to teach big-picture, domain-transferable, abstract concepts from multi-faceted challenges—the kind wisdom needs. Play is practically the only way to accelerate learning of those notions.

If Professor Belcher's work can be characterized as moving from pure lecture to a hybrid lecture-experiential form, then gaming pushes it to pure experience and associated reflection, jettisoning lectures altogether. Gaming is to learning wisdom what lecturing and reading is to acquiring knowledge.

This chapter discusses the value of games for accelerating the experiential learning of wisdom skills. Games are not just ways to improve learner engagement. They also teach concepts that can't be taught well through other mechanisms. They can help novice learners but also serve to capture the wisdom of the experienced. Games are assessment and learning tools at the same time. They not only capture outcomes but also every step of the learning process.

PLAY

Government offices that fund technology development often asked my colleagues and me to help them prioritize investments. Such analyses are complex, requiring the prediction of operational challenges, technical feasibility, impact of the technology, risks and costs to realize those impacts, needed changes to operational paradigms, cultural and other impediments to change, and sensitivity of the answers to each of those assumptions. The answer also needs to be change cognizant. If it's a national security question and the adversary figures out right away how to neutralize the technology, then if not adaptable, the fancy technology could become useless. A technology may need to work across a range of use paradigms and operational missions, but the best solutions may vary for each. The number of variables to consider in such an analysis is enormous.

Scientists can be comfortable with this kind of request when the operational need is clear, humans are at arm's length from the technology, and technology effectiveness can be accurately modeled. For example, early in my career I built an algorithm to detect low-altitude wind patterns around airports that had been crashing airplanes. Well before I developed the software, there needed to be analysis of the ways the wind patterns could be detected. The important measurements were clearly wind speed and direction, and ideally precipitation since the phenomenon is associated with thunderstorms. There are only so many validated ways to measure those weather conditions, and those ways (e.g., RADAR, anemometers) can be accurately modeled. The phenomenon could also be emulated digitally by appropriate weather models. Put those together and a design study could calculate the expected performance of various technologies for detecting the phenomenon. My software used weather RADAR.[133] Another lower-cost system used anemometers.[134]

Analysis of the possibilities gets a whole lot squishier when it's not clear what the technology is specifically trying to help. That's a problem when the decisions of people are involved because people may not recognize the decisions they make or lack understanding of how well they make them (recall the intuitive decision-making discussion).

It is also harder when comparing technologies that help different challenges, which means apples must be compared to oranges. If technology A helps one kind of decision, and technology B helps another, which is the more important need?

Finally, remember the earlier discussion about people not predicting their jobs very well? That's a problem because technologies don't materialize instantly, and the technologies we would analyze were supposed to help over an extended period. There's a prediction aspect. The desire is for operational change because of the technology, and superforecasters or super-users aren't that common. Maybe get the experts together so they can push one another out of imagination troughs? In my experience, good things can happen in those meetings...or it devolves into ego battles. It's not a consistent solution.

One game designer on my team had an idea for making such studies more effective than just listening to experts in a room. The game development team had by then made several games for various uses. One of the lessons was that people's brain cells were tickled a lot by the process of playing. We thought we could give the experts a way to try out technology in an operation using a game. The game approach was called HIVELET (Human-Interactive, Virtual Experimentation for Low-burden Evaluation of Technology).[135]

The game was designed around a question we imagined—"What technologies should be developed for small drones that could transform the effectiveness of dismounted (outside a vehicle) military operations in urban areas?" The game asked a soldier (the player) to find a large drone downed somewhere in a city as quickly and safely as possible.

There were two phases that players iterated on. The first phase was technology selection. The players chose technologies for their small drone (not the downed, large drone they would try to find) from a long list of potential enhancements. They couldn't pick everything as their choices were budget constrained. The second phase was to play a game to find the downed drone with the selected technology's information output. For example, if a sensor to detect warm bodies from a distance was selected for the drone, then the player would get a display of those imagined sensor detections.

The player controlled a character to find the downed drone as quickly as possible without getting shot or shooting noncombatants. They could use any tactics they wished. After completing each few-minute game, the player could pick a different set of technologies and try again. Each scenario varied the downed drone, enemy, noncombatant, and player locations to ensure players wouldn't optimize to a single situation.

Remarkably, the players separately converged on well-performing technology sets within 5-10 game plays (an hour or two). The human brain can be remarkable at whittling a huge number of possibilities down to a small number that make sense, and the players were demonstrating that talent. The best technology choices aren't obvious. Technology mixes can have different utility than each individual one. Sometimes more than one technology is needed for any of them to show value. A technology could help in one scenario but not another. Too much information to game players from prospective technology could overload brains and hurt decision making. Despite those complications, the experts got to a good tech set in a few plays. Better yet...the game exercise wasn't so simple that they arrived at the same answers. They ended up with different mixes and different tactics.

There was collective insight in the converged game solutions. There was commonality in the technologies that players chose. Some of the solutions were imagined ahead of time, but some of the most effective were not, and some of the favorite *a priori* tactics didn't stay favorites. Perhaps most importantly, players were thinking differently after playing. They were more critical of every technology afterward than beforehand.

Psychologists have long studied the benefits of play. There is widespread agreement on its criticality for the development of children[136] and many animals. As Mr. Rogers purportedly said, "Play is often talked about as if it were a relief from serious learning. But for children, play is serious learning."[137] We can't be around children for long without witnessing their insatiable yearning to play.

Yet the benefits of play are not limited to children. Play is useful whenever one wants to get better at "what ifs"—especially ones that are complex, have lots of uncertainties, have multiple, vague, or competing objectives, or involve other actors that are collaborating or competing.

Sure...our brains will naturally do mental simulation to predict outcomes ala what Gary Klein described in his intuitive decision-making model. However, the mental simulation is only as good as our associative concept network and our ability to use that network effectively. The concepts underlying our intuition may be underdeveloped. That's the problem kids have; they simply don't have enough experience to have good intuitions. Play gives them more experiences...even if only imaginary ones.

The typical problems with experiential learning are that it happens slowly and requires the opportunity to have relevant and varied experiences. Play creates experiences that people may never naturally get. Play exposes challenges in a time-evolving way, where at each step the information is incomplete, the challenge might change, and the air drips with uncertainty. That unfolding over time adds richness to what intuition can often offer.

The intuitive process is designed to be fast, but in doing so the memory of the time-evolving experience could be warped. For example, researchers have studied the memory of pain during colonoscopies. The unpleasantness reported after the procedure doesn't correspond to the total amount of pain that patients reported during it. Colonoscopy patients are more likely to retrospectively report the peak pain level or the pain experienced at the end of the procedure.[138] Doctors improved patient's retrospective view of the unpleasant test simply by doing nothing for a while at the end of the procedure.[139] How quickly we forget! The memory isn't absent, but the time-evolving nature of the situation isn't as salient when recalled. The process of going through an evolving situation is different than thinking about it afterward.

The sociality typical of play is a key feature. We don't get other points of view when we're stuck in our own head. Social play creates natural disagreement. It's common to see children fighting about the rules of play or the evolution of a play scenario, for example. Multiple perspectives are key to the learning process.

Play allows us to think counterfactually—a term that refers to the ability to consider possible alternatives to how life events truly work out. When children use fantastical play, they aren't losing touch with reality. They are quite aware that it's make believe. They are analyzing a counterfactual. Research suggests that "individuals high in fantasy proneness have a general tendency to think counterfactually."[140] It's like a scientist testing a theory by reasoning about what would happen if a hypothesis were true. Fantastical play is also a form of analogizing with the real world. Analogies—with their associated abstractions—are a powerful force in creating transferable concepts.[141,142]

The general population's weakness in counterfactual reasoning is on display every day...especially during COVID-19. The oft-displayed inability of the population to understand the importance of a public health measure, or of short-term infection control versus long-term side effects, was limited by their ability to consider what would otherwise happen. Adults should play more!

The HIVELET game provided an explicit way for players to test their intuitions, the experience to correct where it erred, and afterward the socialization to learn from other approaches. Play isn't frivolous; it's serious learning for both adults and children.

My team and I were often asked to explain what games are and what they're not. The definitional debate in the game crowd can obscure a simple answer. Games are vehicles for play, and play can take many forms. All play is an experience, and all experience is instructive in some way...or it can be if we are reflective about it.

As the next section describes, one cool thing about games is they can provide value for both experienced and novice players.

LEVELING UP

I spent twenty years as a leader of tens of high-skill scientists and administrators, and all that time seemed a learning experience. I think learning for that job would never stop. Although I had a lot of help, I was ultimately responsible for getting, mentoring, managing, and occasionally dismissing staff. I had to raise enough money to at least keep them fed (I was at a not-for-profit), cultivate relationships with operators and government decision makers, keep up with several technical fields, develop and present strategic plans and technical results, collaborate with other research groups, and the list goes on.

Nobody can have any one of those responsibilities over twenty years without making plenty of mistakes or sometimes performing suboptimally. Mistakes are more noticeable if there are bad outcomes. Causes could have many origins, such as overwork, time mismanagement, strategic surprise, and interpersonal missteps. Chances are each mistake was a bullet point in some leadership briefing I got, or I was forewarned from more experienced mentors, but nonetheless it didn't hit home until personally experienced.

Is it hopeless, or is there some way for leaders to be better at their jobs more quickly? That seems important for leadership skills since it does seem we have a supply problem. Gallup analysis estimates that only 10% of workers have the native skills to effectively lead.[143]

Beyond leadership—can your job be learned faster? I mean the judgment skills that distinguish the best from the rest—not the mechanics of doing the job. Yes...I think those wisdom skills can be learned faster using games.

One game doesn't have to capture a job's entirety. I'm not talking about the way large game companies go about it, where players navigate complex, highly immersive realms, and many millions of dollars can go into building one game. Players may learn a lot while in such games, but its complexity can mask any one lesson in the same way that real life situations do.

In contrast, games that are purposely for learning are better off trying to isolate an individual lesson...at least at the beginning of a learning progression. It should include some inherent tension, tradeoff, or conflict that requires one or more big-picture judgments.

For example, one of the tensions I observed in my leadership stint is between the short-term performance of a team and its long-term health. New leaders are often the people who were most effective at getting the work done (though of course that shouldn't be the criterion).[144] They are used to being in control. Novice leaders can micromanage, put themselves in a quality-control role overseeing what comes out of the team, or even continue to save some of the more important or pleasurable work for themselves (i.e., trying to be a player-coach). That may succeed in the short-term, but eventually the output of the team can become captive to the bandwidth of the leader.

The leader can burn out, or morale can suffer, resulting in a loss of team productivity and the departure of key personnel. Team creativity and initiative could also suffer. On the other hand, providing too little oversight when team members are inexperienced can result in more mistakes and attendant reputational consequences.

The hardest aspects of designing a game like one about the micromanagement-team empowerment tension I just described is in whittling down to the key aspects of the real world that are relevant for the lesson and devising a way for the game to respond to player actions. Those "game mechanics" are at the heart of what constitutes a game. The complexity of the mechanics should be relative to the skill of the player. If you imagine that at some point the player learns a lesson from the game, then their ability to create an explanation for their decisions is directly tied to their ability to forecast what will happen when they take a game action. If the underlying model of how the game world reacts is too complex for the player's level of understanding, then they could fail to internalize that forecasting model. Alternatively, make the model too simple for what players already have in their heads, and they could be bored or—worse yet—find the game implausible. It's hard to get it right the first time, so the best game design process tends to be highly iterative. It's why I'm not proposing a micromanagement-team empowerment game design in this text; the first attempt at the design won't likely be the final one (see the section on Agile processes in Chapter 8).

Gamers are accustomed to the notion of "leveling up"—a progression to a greater difficulty level. That notion is also valid for wisdom-oriented games, but unlike for entertainment games, the relative simplicity and transparency of learning games offers a lot of additional leveling-up opportunities. Maybe a lower level of a Team Oversight game (the micromanagement-team empowerment topic) has a leader-centric focus where the leader's time management is on center stage and issues of team morale and creativity are absent. Many situational variants could be presented in that Level 1. Ideally those variants would demand a different balance between team success and leader micromanagement. Iteration over varied situations helps learners generalize the lesson. Higher game levels could incrementally introduce other factors such as additional objectives (morale, turnover) or constraints (team skill composition).

That's the conventional notion of leveling up, but it can be extended further. A goal in learning wisdom should be to get players to the point that they can impact the design of future games. In doing so, they progress from student to teacher. That can take simple forms to start, such as including an additional factor in the game mechanics or a new scenario type that requires different player considerations. Over time, it can mean designing a game from scratch—likely with other gurus.

The design of a game is a complex endeavor that should involve the wisest members of an organization. Game design requires a series of judgments about the essence of situations, decisions, assumptions, constraints, mechanisms, and influences, and the important heuristics or tradeoffs that should be teaching points. Expert game designer Dr. Robert Seater at MIT Lincoln Lab (who invented the HIVELET technique) wrote a superb book chapter that describes the important considerations in the complicated business of educational game design that I highly recommend.[145] The process itself is a wisdom spreader. It forces difficult conversations about what matters most in the game—and by extension in the real-life job—that may not otherwise occur. Game design is the ultimate leveling up, but the beneficiaries aren't only the players. They're the organization, job type, or industry. The design is hugely valuable regardless of whether the game gets built.

Building a game doesn't necessarily mean high expense or software gurus. Games don't have to be computerized. If they are, they may not need fancy graphics for the learning objective. If software needs to be built, then emerging technology is making it possible for end users to develop game software without coding skill.[146,147] Many people have already had ChatGPT build a game for them. Game development—like AI—is also democratizing.

Promoting the use of games can conjure visions of student heads buried endlessly in computer screens. That isn't what I'm imagining. Playing a game should be a minority of the learning time. The rest would include deep dives to shore up knowledge deficits that students need to play the game well. Remember...we shouldn't abandon detailed or more narrow conceptual knowledge but rather teach it as needed for learning a big-picture lesson. Reflection before and after game play is also critical for bringing intuitive lessons to conscious awareness.

Leveling up in wisdom games can involve the wise and the as-yet unwise.

GAMES HELP EDUCATION RESEARCH

A few years ago, I led a grant proposal to the U.S. Department of Education. It was ill-fated, but that was expected. Grant proposals to the U.S. government have typical success rates in the 10-20% range, and I was not published or otherwise known in education circles (reputation matters since other education researchers judge the proposals).

It was always a long shot. Instead, I want to focus on how that grant proposal illustrated some broader problems.

For many years, the notion of Computational Thinking (CT) has been permeating elementary and middle school classrooms.[148] CT teaches basic principles of computer programming—decomposition, pattern recognition/data representation, generalization/abstraction, and algorithms—by integrating those principles in a student's typical coursework and applying them to a variety of real-world topics. Basically, kids are taught about formulating problems, breaking them into pieces, and devising step-by-step solutions. Those are hugely important skills for coding and everyday life.

We proposed a new course that would teach an analogous but also pragmatic complement to CT. I called it Decision Thinking. The purpose was to teach the underlying principles of AI in ways that were general enough to apply outside of AI. The elements of the proposed course included sections on:

- Decision mapping: What decisions are needed to solve a problem better?
- Performance measures: How does one know a good decision from a bad one?
- Data transform: What goes into and comes out of a decision, and how is that information represented?
- Optimality: What does "best" mean and what are strategies to find the optimum?
- Decision principles: How are decisions made, and what do the decisions mean?
- Decision context: What is context and how does it affect decisions?

- Using decisions: How should decisions be interpreted, and responses be chosen?

In my mind, the bulk of the proposed work should be in designing the course, but that's not how it ended up. As is typical for education research, the required emphasis was on evaluating the course.[149] Care was taken to define student groups who would test the course, to design appropriate experimental controls, and to reduce the data bias from atypical teaching quality. It was also required that an independent entity design and perform the assessment.

I understand the scientific rationale for proving the course value, but we weren't proposing to replace an existing course. The material wasn't otherwise taught. What exactly are the success criteria? Isn't some learning on a high-priority topic better than none? It felt ass backward. Decide whether to adopt the course content or not based on its inherent importance...however smart minds define that. Then figure out how to optimize the learning.

There was an even bigger problem. The whole process—design, course conduct, and analysis of results—would take four years. Four years to affect a portion of one school district, after which it would take several more years to convince other schools to adopt it. I was looking at a decade or so before this important topic maybe affects a fraction of the country.

Educational research has a time-scale problem. If we wait until we have proof of an intervention, then we're waiting a long time. By the time the proof exists, the world has changed—maybe changed a ton in a field like AI. The relevance of the research question could have changed a lot too. A decade for an AI-related subject felt like forever.

Big educational shifts won't happen without taking a few judgment leaps before there is proof.

Games offer a richer and faster way to understand learning utility. They are simultaneously the teaching tool and the test. We just need to rethink what proficiency means. For conventional schooling, the barometers are tests that are at a separate time from the learning. We learn, then we test. With gaming, performance is what the player accomplishes—like how performance is evaluated at work. Games are testing tools because they measure what people can do in the face of particular challenges. Like for performance in the workplace, the key is the result. Progressing in game levels is like a girl or boy scout badge for an accomplishment. Badges are pitched as an empowering alternative to traditional grading.[150]

It gets better. If the games are computerized, then perhaps for the first time in education history the entire learning process is captured—every decision a learner makes and the conditions and outcomes associated with each decision. Game-based experiential learning can be a treasure trove for investigating how wisdom concepts are learned.

Game data could then be used to transform learning pedagogies. Perhaps a learner does best when they take more risk in initial game plays and fill out their mental model faster. Maybe learning is accelerated by mixing in a more difficult scenario early on to give learners a glimpse of what's coming and get their unconscious mind chewing on it. Perhaps those who took a different game, or who had a certain prior course, or were different in myriad individual ways, could get their game badge faster than others. The range of analysis questions on the best learning conditions—perhaps to as fine a granularity as individual learners—is practically boundless.

I don't love how school is driven so much by standardized tests; nor do many in education. Nevertheless, I don't think they're going away. If we're going to have such evaluations, then some of them should be games that attempt to measure wisdom-related skill. The data will illuminate how students approach experiential learning, and potentially how to optimize learning paths.

§

Computer games evoke pushbacks in much of the population. Studies and influential opinions point to the dangers of increased screen time, of youth overindulgence in gaming at the expense of healthier activities, at the addictive qualities of entertainment games, and of violent or sexualized game content. I do not dispute the importance of those issues, but I'm also trying to differentiate from entertainment games.

Screen time is an issue that extends way beyond gaming. Computers are a medium—not a specific activity. The trouble is that so many of the uses of computers (including smartphones) are on sites whose business model is all about getting and keeping a user's attention. Once grabbed, the attention beast delivers increasingly extreme or overamplified content. It's a huge issue I don't dispute, and entertainment games can be part of the problem.

Yet there are redeeming educational features of many games.[151] One of my kids became fond of the game Minecraft. It is a sandbox game without specific goals. Players try to change a virtual world by building things out of a range of virtual materials (e.g., stone, dirt, even lava). They can be trying to get their character to survive or play the entire game in a creative mode with no consequences to anything they do. My daughter built complex structures in this virtual world—a task differing only in scale and medium from playing with Legos or Lincoln Logs. While parents may dwell on shoot-em-up aspects of entertainment games, many games involve role playing and strong socialization aspects. Players are required to exercise social skills and explicitly strategize to accomplish goals. They are playing, and play is a learning construct. Some of what they learn will be more generally useful. We should work harder to understand those transferable skills.

Far, far away from the gaming realm lies digitized education. It is layered upon the attention economy...in that both use computers...and in my view that intersection can be a problem. Most educators deliver the same material and assessments as before—only through a computer instead of pencil and paper. There are efficiencies in doing so, but I would expect degraded learning in the process. Delivering lectures via computer weakens the interpersonal connection that comes with in-person instruction. The engagement level of the educational material (mostly lectures) is no rival to what's going on elsewhere on the computer. It competes with the distractions from more engaging or addictive computer-based options. Internet-based instruction and its ability to reach students around the globe has struggled with the reality that it is much harder to stay engaged and complete courses online than it is in person. Completion rates for adult online courses are abysmal.[152]

We can blame the computer medium, or we can address the engagement issue. Why should learning be a slog?

Learning for me can be highly engrossing...addictive even. I mentioned the Rubik's Cube phase of my childhood. I taught myself how to solve it consistently in under a minute, and along the way I could barely put it down. Great books can do the same. Even my historical disdain for writing has been cracked. Sometimes I can even get into an enjoyable flow state when typing away...with total immersion in the material and the rest of the world barely sensed. Learning can be joyful; it shouldn't hurt.

Learner engagement comes from being challenged by interesting problems at just the right level of difficulty. Too hard and the struggle is discouraging; too easy and it is boring. The objective of games for learning shouldn't be engagement; it should be in creating interesting challenges. Engagement will follow.

Unfortunately, educational games have largely focused on engagement. That's seemingly because of both a trickle-down effect of the entertainment game industry and because the games are going after the wrong types of learning goals.

By 2020, entertainment gaming was generating more worldwide revenue than any other media except TV; more than books, newspapers, movies, radio, music (live and recorded), and streaming movies.[153] It's so much money that the major companies don't have much incentive to address a less lucrative education market. There are game companies specifically devoted to education, but collectively they have not impacted schools in any major way.

Games for education are hyped to educators, but the promise is stunted by the reality that many of them aren't very good. If educators see enough of that, then the very mention of games can bring more eye-rolling than interest.

The primary problem is that the games are trying to improve knowledge transfer or grow domain-specific concepts. This is largely because that's what the educational market allows. Schools insist that new tools address their curriculum mandates, and those are to teach kids how to solve math problems, learn details about history, or learn to read, for example. Schools want games to deliver detail, but there's no reason to believe that games are a good mechanism for that.

As a result, game companies tout engagement as the principal benefit. A kid can still be bored to tears learning algebra, but a sweetener is added in the form of embedding the lesson in a game. The result often doesn't work. A fantasy realm where players must stop and solve equations periodically isn't taking advantage of what games can do best. Sure...kids will learn detailed information from games, but that detail sticks if it's integral to a larger experience that's challenging, and if the detail matters for that challenge.

There is a more important benefit than creating engagement. Gaming is key because it can teach things that can't be learned nearly as well in other ways. They can teach big-picture, abstract concepts that modern work demands...not detail. As the HIVELET downed-drone game illustrated, it can expose unconscious thinking, bringing it toward insight. It can measure as well as teach. It allows failure, rethinking, and retrying that neither conventional schooling nor real life are very tolerant of. Games are a medium for iteratively experiencing using self-directed discovery. It is the challenge that engages a learner—not lipstick on a pig in the form of fancy graphics, or a fantasy world on top of an otherwise boring problem.

Wisdom skills cannot be easily taught by the explicit instruction of conventional classrooms. Real-life experience takes too long and isn't diverse enough. Play seems to have emerged in evolution to deal with that gap. Games should be applied to teaching wisdom skills instead of expertise ones.

Professor Belcher's TEAL paradigm represents the best of expertise instruction, using a hybrid of explicit instruction (lectures), social sharing, hands-on project work, frequent feedback, and as many ways of explaining as possible. TEAL has as much in common with playing as with lecturing because the intent is to convey understanding of concepts instead of detailed knowledge. Yet the concepts are for precise phenomena in a narrow context. Throw some human beings or other forms of uncertainty into the mix, or situational factors that could completely change the interpretations, and the lecture part becomes nearly useless. Those challenges require gaming.

Life teaches lessons if we pay attention and want to learn, but life takes a long time. It relies on the opportunity to have the experiences, including some we shouldn't want to have, as they're painful. Life doesn't give us a do-over. Games aren't real life but they're a complementary vehicle to the slow journey we're on. They should have a lofty place for work-related experiential learning comparable at least to apprenticeships, project-based learning, and case studies.

I've identified a key tool—games—but what good is a proverbial hammer if there are no nails to pound. Schooling is stuck in a different modality that...as the next chapter describes...is diametrically opposed to the best conditions for learning wisdom.

7.

UPSIDE-DOWN SCHOOLING

We get so thoroughly used to a kind of pseudo-idea, a half perception, that we are not aware how half-dead our mental action is, and how much keener and more extensive our observations and ideas would be if we formed them under conditions of a vital experience which required us to use judgement: to hunt for the connections of the thing dealt with.

John Dewey[154]

Horace Mann got himself out of poverty by educating himself using the public library in his hometown Franklin, Massachusetts.[155] It was the first book-lending public library in the U.S.—started with books gifted by Benjamin Franklin.

Horace had little formal schooling in his youth, but as an adult he graduated as valedictorian from Brown University. He became a lawyer and spent a decade in the Massachusetts legislature before his legacy role began in 1837 as the state's first Education Secretary.

It was there he made his biggest mark. By the time he left for the U.S. House of Representatives in 1858, Horace had transformed schooling in Massachusetts. Other states followed the Massachusetts model. It isn't an exaggeration to say that the residue of Mann's model still affects modern U.S. primary and secondary education.

His principles for mass education are summarized as:

1. "[T]he public should no longer remain ignorant;

2. [T]hat such education should be paid for, controlled, and sustained by an interested public;
3. [T]hat this education will be best provided in schools that embrace children from a variety of backgrounds;
4. [T]hat this education must be non-sectarian;
5. [T]hat this education must be taught using the tenets of a free society; and
6. [T]hat education should be provided by well-trained, professional teachers."[156]

This sounds no-brainer to us, but the notions were controversial for their time. For most countries in Europe, education was a privilege of the elite—not a right of the common person—for another hundred years. Mann was saying everyone should be educated, whether boy or girl, white or not.[157] He said that government should pay for it, that it should be open to various religious beliefs (note he wasn't saying it should be free of religion), and that teachers should be trained.

Mass education was the law in Massachusetts and many other states before Mann took the reins, but its implementation had many problems. Each community got to decide how it would educate its people, and many towns weren't putting energy into it. Often local governments would pay the fines for not having a public school rather than pay to form one.[158] Teachers weren't selected based on their competence. Whoever was free to do it—or maybe were lucky enough to get a patronage job—would teach.

Schools would teach what they wished. They often opted for highly religious instruction in keeping with the priority of education for the first couple of centuries of colonial life. Top priority was being able to read the Bible, though the burgeoning Catholic population didn't like schools' Protestant leanings. Mann was a Unitarian—a

Protestant sect with a more liberal theology than others—but he was religious. The second priority was reading laws and other civic duties.

It was this hodgepodge of school offerings that Mann sought to control with structure and standards. He was not alone. Mann was in the Whig party with other school reform advocates that sought a degree of centralization. However, the Democrats and much of the country still preferred local autonomy.

He looked internationally for good models. In 1843, Horace traveled to Great Britain and Prussia. It was the Prussian model that enamored him as it had other reformers.

Prussia controlled a wide swath of land in current-day Germany, Poland, Russia, and Denmark. It is historically renowned for its military prowess and precision. Prussia ordered attendance of all children at state schools in 1717 under King Frederick William I. They were the first country to institute mass education.[159]

By the time of Horace Mann, Frederick the Great (Frederick II) was Prussia's ruler. Though full of apparent contradictions according to today's moralities, Frederick the Great was a different kind of ruler for his day. He was a big catalyst for the Enlightenment. His philosophy was that rulers should make their subjects happy. I don't think I can say that about many modern rulers and politicians!

He announced in public that "Our grand care will be further the Country's well-being, and to make every one of our subject[s] contented and happy. Our will is, not that you strive to enrich us by vexation of our subjects; but rather you aim steadily as well towards that advantage of the country..."[160] He meant it. In his first winter of rule... amid a famine...Frederick sold much of the government's grain to the poor at decent rates. He created a less corruptible and harsh justice system than in other kingdoms. Not a very religious man, he encouraged religious tolerance, writing "...in this country every man must get to heaven in his own way."[160]

Frederick's benevolence didn't extend to Prussia's neighbors, nor should his treatment of the poor be mistaken for democratic leanings. He was a strict disciplinarian and believer in despotic rule but saw content people as less likely to revolt.

His father had built a finely tuned, highly effective army. Frederick the Great—drilled in military arts in childhood (against his more artistic desires)—leveraged the army for territorial gain throughout his reign. He became known as one of history's great military tacticians.[161]

Prussian education intended to create a great army first and foremost. Everything about Prussian governance was oriented around precision, organization, and other militaristic leanings. One historian and teacher described Prussia as "an army with a country."[162] Frederick believed that educated soldiers were better soldiers. Mass education probably did help the Prussian military distribute decision making to lower ranks. That allowed improvisation in local situations, and that was a big part of their success. Make no mistake though—Frederick the Great wasn't trying to create free thinkers.

When Horace Mann selected the Prussian education model, he chose a structure of single-age classrooms (instead of grouping by ability), a professionally trained teacher corps taught to teach the same material in the same ways (often with rote memorization), and precisely timed, fixed-duration class periods. Subjects and courses carved by knowledge domains became another structural feature when secondary schools emerged later in the 19th century. Those characteristics still define most schools.

Mann instantiated a school system with principles that were hotly debated along political and religious boundaries, but it may have been the wisest path for that time. Unfortunately, we're still living with the Prussian structure, and it no longer fits. A yearning for school uniformity and the filling of heads with detail still reigns.

Some derisively call it the factory model of education, with allusion to the Industrial Revolution. I play on that in the *Wisdom Factories* title of the book. The biggest connotations of the factory model terminology are that each child is taught the same things in the same way, that schools are run with precision and a top-down ethos, and that the education subjects learn to be docile factory workers.

It is unfair to call modern schooling a factory model. Despite the sense among the public that little has changed, a lot has. I am not telling the Horace Mann story—one most educators have heard too many times—to claim lack of educational evolution. Since my school days, there has been an increased emphasis on conceptual understanding over rote memorization, much more focus on individual student needs, application of learning science in how material is taught, and recognition that non-academic aspects of school are also critical for child development.

However, attitudes, ethos, and structure are more pervasive constraints, and those have been slower to change. It is in that spirit that I bring up Horace.

I have talked about the importance of wisdom skills, explained that it focuses on big-picture concepts that are learned experientially, and described games as a key tool in accelerating experience. Great...so more games in school...right?

It's not that simple. Emphasizing wisdom changes the whole paradigm. Absolutely everything must be reconsidered: the learning approach, curriculum, school structure, the roles of teachers and students, and perhaps most importantly, society's attitudes.

Wisdom schooling feeds the right hemisphere and intuitive portions of our brains. It encourages the growth of central, abstract concepts in our brain's associative network. It is driven by experiential learning on complex challenges that's supplemented by knowledge learning. Those differences have a radical impact on nearly everything about schooling. They require an education model that flips the existing paradigm upside down.

There is nothing sacred about how things are done now. New challenges demand open-minded approaches. It's time we stopped doing things because it's always the way we've done things. The Prussians no longer have anything to teach us.

STUDENT AGENCY

I went to a small Catholic elementary school that didn't have its own library. We used the "bookmobile"—a sixteen-wheeler that came to school often. I visited the bookmobile one day and had a specific goal. It was 1972, on the tail end of the Apollo moon missions. I was jazzed about outer space. There was lots of information on the planets, but one that I couldn't find much about. I was hunting for a Pluto book.

Before long I had my prize, and it wasn't some skimpy book. It was thick and wordy and more than a bit intimidating, but I was determined. The librarian who checked me out questioned whether I could handle it. "Are you sure you want this book?" she said. "Yes," I assured her, and to her credit she didn't get in the way of my passion.

I took it home and began to read. I must have labored over the first pages of text for over an hour, going back to repeat paragraphs and sentences that seemed to go on forever. I was kind of getting the point (so my adult brain says), but I still didn't have any idea what it had to do with Pluto.

It didn't. I had misread the title. The book was Plato's *Republic*. The word Plato was splashed across the cover in giant letters. In my excitement I hadn't noticed the single-letter difference. I was so disappointed!

Never underestimate a child's yearning to understand and to impact the real world (and what lies beyond it). I have asked many adults about their big school influences and what academics they remember most. They often describe a teacher of course, and they inevitably describe special projects where they got to choose the topic or exert some of their own influence on what they were learning. I personally remember the multi-week school projects, but a very small fraction of the daily classroom stuff. I remember learning lots, but not what I learned. I didn't care enough or use the information enough for it to stick.

It is widely recognized that student engagement in learning is a driver of many positive outcomes.[163] It is also known that student engagement stinks in the U.S., decreasing steadily from fifth grade (three-quarters are engaged) to the end of high school (about one-third is engaged).[164]

Engagement isn't attention. It's how much students are psychologically invested in learning the material...independent of grading. Teacher quality can be an enormous influence on engagement of course, but so can their intrinsic motivations driven by interest, relevance, and impact. The best teacher of material a student doesn't care about will only bring engagement part way.

Engagement should always be a priority, but it has amplified importance in wisdom-focused schooling. The right brain is more interest driven than the left brain, though that might be an oversimplification. Both hemispheres have interests, but the left brain is interested in drilling down given a topic or task. The right brain is allergic to being dutiful. Its primary need is to seek meaning, consistency, and completeness. It doesn't readily pursue someone else's interest.

Duty was a big part of student life when mass education began, and that ethos is still pervasive. I get the need for school to have an organization, standards and norms, and other practices that create a learning environment. However, an underlying duty vibe can permeate the nature of the material taught and the pedagogies applied.

Many parents have told me they think instilling work ethic is a primary purpose of schooling. The voluminous homework doesn't concern them, nor that their kids won't remember most of what they're learning. They seem unconcerned that much of the learning material will never be used in adulthood. In their minds, it's the process of working hard that matters. Students need to slog through boring work and pay attention.

Colleges pile onto the duty pressure of high school students. They want students to "show evidence that they are challenging themselves"—a mantra I heard at every college tour I attended with my kids. The translation for students and parents is "show us you'll oversubscribe yourself and be chronically sleep-deprived."

The emphasis on duty was imprinted on me in high school in the 80s. My cross-country team coach approached me one day after practice. He asked why I didn't pay attention in his trigonometry class. I respected coach a lot; he was a good man and teacher, and he spoke to me pleasantly. He was right—I didn't pay attention much. Sometimes I was doing the homework for the next class that I hadn't bothered to do the night before. I often daydreamed or half-slept, even though I liked math. I behaved similarly in other classes. Most of my teachers let me get away with it since I aced their tests and assignments, but this teacher wanted more.

He wanted to see me working hard, commenting that I need to develop the skill of...apparently...putting high energy into something. I responded—also pleasantly—that "I will work hard when it is necessary." It was flippant, but I didn't understand the criticism. I was acing his class, too. "What about the time I spent at home immersed in puzzles or reading books, often for hours of deep concentration," I thought. "What about enduring the pain of a hard workout or race, which he witnessed daily? Is it my fault he's not challenging me?"

That experience was a long time ago, but attitudes can take generations to change. A nose-to-the-grindstone attitude still survives...with enormous implications.

It imposes an increasingly dour school vibe as the grade levels increase. Kids know their fun time is going away, even before they encounter high-workload grades.

Grading systems are a factor. Having the work judged can negatively affect engagement—even before the judgment is rendered. The feeling of being judged is demotivating.[165]

By the time people are adults, many of them feel that learning is work, not fun. If anything should come out of all those years of schooling, it should be joy in learning and knowledge of the best learning practices. The conditions of boredom, lack of student agency, and shallow, detail-oriented learning drain students' natural energy. All that remains is duty.

Wanting students to have grit doesn't mean prescribing unquestioning duty. Imposing it externally runs counter to the self-confidence at the core of grit. It's also antithetical to critical thinking. Keeping a brain in a dutiful state will block us from breaking out of a well-worn thought mode.

Duty for a good reason is sensible, but it's always accompanied by a loss of agency. Natural reactions to being controlled are to give in—thereby suspending critical thinking—to internalize resentment, or to rebel. Duty for duty's sake can lead to myopia and manipulation. It can suppress creativity and independent thinking. The dutiful are more easily duped.

A duty-oriented environment may have made sense when employers wanted employees who would do what they are told and labor on mindlessly repetitive work. Every job can feel that way at times, but more often modern employees are asked to solve problems with minimal direction.

It's easy to take baby steps that let student agency and interest percolate the environment. There are lots of part-way solutions from "every student learns what we tell them to learn" to "each student learns what it wants." There's a sliding scale from locked-down to anarchy.

The left brain can handle being told what to do. The right brain wants to free think. Emphasizing wisdom means allowing student choice about aspects of their learning journey—engagement over duty.

Another aspect of engagement is in posing challenges that naturally invoke students' interest and sense of relevance and importance. Those will be problems that are complex (age-appropriately) and are posed experientially.

COMPLEX, EXPERIENTIAL CHALLENGES

It was the lack of progress in school achievement and their belief in the power of engagement that in 2008 got educators at Apple, Inc. to propose a very different kind of paradigm—Challenge-Based Learning.[166] The philosophy is simple. Instead of drilling students on details that may someday come together and be used to solve a real-world problem, why not have students address a real-world problem right away? Starting from a big idea—perhaps flying to the moon or reducing child hunger—students would whittle it down to manageable ideas and sub-elements about which the students had some say. Then they would try to solve the challenge to some degree, if only in their neighborhood or sliver of the problem space.

The results were stunning.[167] After two studies involving 1500 students from 24 schools in 3 countries, both students and teachers were highly positive of Challenge-Based Learning. Three-quarters of students felt they worked harder than they normally do, learned more than what they were required to, and felt like they were doing something important. A similar fraction of teachers felt the students mastered the material and their students' engagement increased. About 90% of the teachers felt the approach was worth their time, and that 21st-Century Skills were improved significantly. Those improvements were in creativity, leadership, problem solving, collaboration, initiative, and adaptability.

Workers need to solve problems...often big ones...and people don't learn to solve big problems without practicing solving big problems.

Wisdom-based learning, and experiential learning in general, starts from a challenge premise. Learning of detail is purpose-driven and on-demand, enabling a problem solver to chip away at a solution.

That process should be familiar to professionals. The problem comes first. Work challenges inevitably involve complexities requiring other perspectives and skills. Knowledge is pulled in as needed to address the problem. People decide what learning is needed, find authoritative sources, and keep moving. To do anything else—to learn all about chemistry when one needs most to understand antibodies, for example—would be downright silly. Who has time for that? Tomorrow there will be another challenge with a different knowledge need. I remember when I had to learn new computer languages. It was great to have the manual, and I may have skimmed it before starting, but the best way to learn the language was to start building stuff.

Let me give an example. Suppose the learning intent is teaching intuitive concepts related to resource allocation. That could include a hedging-the-bet concept from an earlier chapter. Ideally the instruction would have students doing resource management under various conditions and in different application areas. Remember, variation is important. My teams developed games of this sort related to transportation, emergency response, and military operations. I could imagine many other applications, from the time management of students' daily lives, resources of ecosystems and organisms, and...yes...travel in outer space (without Plato this time). The variety of applications would allow students to choose games of interest to them that address the same learning goals, and later test the transferability of the learned concepts to other realms.

In teaching about resource management, students could be led to dive deeply into relevant knowledge areas. That could include historical case studies of the impact of great and poor allocation. Maybe there's a discussion of common biases of human decision making such as the tendency to solve the short-term allocation problem and leave the long-term one a mess. There could be units on recognizing trade-offs and the math associated with them. It could discuss why resource management problems are often extremely difficult to solve, and how AI optimization systems help decision makers in many industries. In learning wisdom, the challenge is the central organizer—not the knowledge discipline.

Students should try to solve challenges—not only think about them. Retrospective case studies have their place, as do projects that practice processes toward a known answer. However, only in trying to solve complex challenges are the intricacies and wisdom lessons fully revealed. Experiential learning means going through a process of experiencing, not being told about an experience, or being given the lessons in a briefing chart. The challenges should be complex enough that they can be at least partially solved, that progress can be measured in multiple ways, and that there are inherent tensions or tradeoffs.

There isn't a better means for delivering complex challenges than games. Students are put in specific situations, including ones they can't experience in the real world. They are asked to devise answers to the situational problems by making a series of decisions subject to rules or constraints. They get feedback on how well they're doing. That, folks, is another way of defining a game.

Gee...doesn't that sound like the conditions in a conventional essay assignment, for example? In those assignments, students are asked to devise answers with rules and constraints given by the teacher, and they get feedback in the form of a grade. Why isn't that a game? The philosophical hairs to split are whether the conditions of play are present...like the allowance of failures on the way to success, and whether the nature of the feedback is adequately mappable to student actions. Then...sure...I guess it's a game, even though the amount of iteration in any essay writing assignment is limited.

Whether the game is computerized or not is a choice, but it doesn't take much thinking to see the advantages of digitization. If a computer doesn't provide the feedback, then a person must—

probably the teacher. That limits the amount and types of feedback. Teacher bandwidth could limit the number and variability of game challenges. Computer games capture information on how a player gets to a solution and can even ask questions during the game to check conceptual understanding. That provides data to inform game design changes, the content of the next knowledge deep dive, or even the challenge progressions. Computer games also allow for the creation of AI tutors that can help novice players get unstuck. Many education game tutors have already been developed.

The detail-first pedagogy of schools is driven by historical momentum, the ease of delivering the content uniformly to all students, and the simplicity of testing what was learned. Wisdom-based learning requires more tools.

The first principle of educating for wisdom is to prioritize student agency. The second is to organize teaching around complex, multidisciplinary challenges.

The third principle may be the hardest for the education system to swallow. You may have spotted the issue already. Where exactly in the curriculum would teaching something like resource management...as a general competency...fit in? How one divides up wisdom competencies is going to be very different from how expertise learning is divided up. The curriculum will have to change.

A WISDOM CURRICULUM

Teaching via big-picture challenges will immediately run into some practical roadblocks. For one, school time is neatly carved up into small time blocks according to disciplinary divisions—language, math, science, social studies, art, etc. At the K-12 level, each subject has to teach mandated knowledge and concepts. Real-world challenges won't fit neatly into those disciplinary silos.

There are other desirable wisdom-oriented features. Class length could need adjustment. Addressing a big challenge means giving children enough uninterrupted time to really dig in. Socialization is crucial during the learning process. That can mean collaborating with students in other classrooms or grades who have similar interests or other perspectives.

In other words, a new teaching philosophy oriented around wisdom will run up against the structural constraints of schooling that was designed for knowledge stuffing: specific, declared subjects based on knowledge categories; single-age classrooms; short and fixed time periods; and prescribed and enforced content. Hello Prussian system!

Let's start with the basic curriculum questions. Are we teaching the most important material, and how do we define what's most important? Is school organized around those learning goals?

School has never been entirely about preparing kids for jobs; it's also about getting them ready to be informed and constructive members of society. Whether explicitly or not, they learn values and ideals—like in how to treat other people.

However, regardless of the educational purpose, the need for wisdom is the same. The same factors that drive the need for wisdom in the workplace also apply to life outside work. Parenting and romantic relationships are more complex, too, and there's abundant evidence that voters are often viewing complex issues through an overly simple, bumper-sticker lens. I recognize that school isn't all about a future job, but quibbling about which purpose is more important is a red herring. The value of wisdom doesn't start at the workplace door. Ways of thinking always bleed across the boundaries.

I think the debate about what to teach is a misguided one if premised by a challenge-independent perspective. Too often the conversation degrades to arguments that rely upon dubious assumptions. One is that if a category of knowledge is important, then everything taught under it must be. Another is that knowledge is important if it is relevant to some adults—abandoning the notion of relative value. The argument of last resort is often that the specific knowledge being taught might not be very useful, but it teaches a key thinking skill. That too lacks a relative comparison with other options, as the skill might be taught in other ways.

That's how curriculum topics become immovable—almost sacred—because the arguments, if devoid of a discussion of what is most useful, devolve into versions of "it can't hurt." It does hurt. Education time is precious. Kids can tell if something is irrelevant to them. One need only look at the debate around cursive writing instruction to see how silly it becomes. How often do digitally connected people write by hand anymore? If they do, print writing is just as fast as cursive writing. Cursive was invented to minimize blotting from feather pens and ink wells!

I don't have the answers to which subjects are most important at what ages, but if one takes a challenge-oriented view—if wisdom is the paramount consideration—then there are two rules of thumb for determining them. Every wisdom course should be relevant to every person's future (in K-12), and the curriculum must connect to the most prevalent needs for addressing real-life challenges. With those criteria I would bet psychology and sociology rise near the top, as would computer and data sciences, complex systems, logic and rhetoric, interpersonal strategies, search and discovery, processes for enhancing creativity and collaboration, problem formulation, and information vetting. I didn't work too hard on that list, but each of those are drowned out of most current curricula.

I could also drone on about other school dogma. Grouping kids together by age, while socially important, makes it impossible to serve the cognitive needs of every student. Many get left behind while others are held back. With respect to grading, studies show rewards for achievement are more motivating than punishment for errors.[168] That does not mean giving everyone a trophy. Rather, it means allowing failure along the learning journey.

Most lists of 21st-Century Skills include the four C's—critical thinking, creativity, communication, and collaboration—plus adaptability, leadership, and information and computing emphases. Two decades later, where are the high school classes on each of these subjects? When do we explicitly teach every student about interpersonal interaction and understanding others, for example?

Even a knowledge discipline add-on like computer science has been poorly served. Almost half of U.S. high schools don't offer a single Computer Science (CS) course.[169] Only 5.6% of high school students are enrolled in a CS course.[169] One reason given is not enough teachers with computer science skills. The system has had plenty of time for teacher skills to catch up, and don't tell me industry CS jobs are stealing teachers. Being capable of teaching Computer Science does not make one a great CS worker and vice-versa.

It is hard to think we're serious about 21st-Century Skills when each of those skills includes a rich body of knowledge, processes, and intriguing dilemmas, but courses, standards, and accountability measures relevant to those skills are scarce. I'll know we're making progress in this tough transition from an expertise to a wisdom model when there are instructors that define themselves as experts in critical thinking or collaboration!

The canons of modern schooling deserve rethinking as part of any reform. Many of them haven't been revisited...outside of a few vanguard schools that affect relatively few students...since the days of Horace Mann.

§

Horace Mann and the Prussian system is the progenitor of what became called the factory model of education. That label connotes shallow learning of detail and uniform content for each student. It is a disparaging comparison to Industrial Revolution mass production that implies the impersonal manufacturing of workers.

What we need now are *Wisdom Factories*. That may seem oxymoronic since wisdom feels opposite to cookie-cutter factories. A modern factory is full of machines, uses workers to manage the machines and adapt them creatively to new needs, and produces a lot of something. That's the spirit of the word factories in the book title.

Pasting wisdom intentions on top of a system designed to produce expertise simply won't work. It hasn't. Placing highest priority on wisdom must come with paradigm shifts.

The needed shifts are cascading. One change begets another. Increasing student agency, if done properly, will lead schools toward complex, multidisciplinary challenges that drive student curiosities. Addressing such challenges can only get sufficient prominence through a major reworking of curricula.

At the highest level, learning wisdom is upside down from learning expertise. Instead of details and a disciplinary focus, it's big picture and multidisciplinary.

Transforming schools to prioritize wisdom would be the most fundamental system change since the formation of mass education.

There are many schools that demonstrate aspects of a wisdom paradigm, but none that I know of that have gone so far as I propose. Montessori schools, for example, have long placed experiential learning above knowledge stuffing, but they are constrained in how big picture the experiences can be because of standardized tests and college desires. Some schools have emphasized more student choice, or challenge-based learning, or have introduced interdisciplinary subjects. However, few have done all three at once. New paradigms are constrained by structure, standards, and attitudes.

I know these are huge changes. I also know there are huge obstacles to change. I am not naïve. These conversations will be difficult. The required mindset change is dramatic. Everyone will be unhappy with the changes for a while, even if they agree with my philosophies. It won't be comfortable, and human beings like comfort.

These changes will also rub against the expectations in the population that learning is measured by what knowledge students remember. It means some of the knowledge that has historically been taught will have to go. No longer should the battle be about what specific knowledge to stuff into kids because "after all they gotta know that to be adults." Clearly, we're already leaving lots off the list that others like me would argue they gotta know. Knowledge has exploded; we're not going to transfer it all to any brain—child or adult. Your list of important knowledge may or may not be better than my list, but arguing about the list is off the mark. There are choices to make. The only way to pivot is to leave some things behind. Where there is a universal learning need, it is because the capability is important to every profession. Those will be conceptual, big-picture skills, not detailed knowledge.

Schools are stuck. Most discussions focus on tweaks when remodeling is needed. Changes are add-ons to an already overloaded agenda. Some topics have become dogma or third rails and are not subject to alternative thinking at all. Much of the U.S. believes that schools are incapable of changing.

We must change. That onus is on business and society as well as schools. There is too much at stake to cling to an outdated model. In the final chapter I talk about how to grease the wheels of change.

First though, there is one topic I have glazed over so far. Remember Mona—the fictional psychotherapist from the first chapter? She had to manage her AI team. That task will be a big part of most jobs. The next chapter describes the skills and tools for managing the AI team.

8.

PRODUCTIVITY THERAPY

The rise of intelligent AI assistants...means everyone will become the manager of their own team of artificially intelligent machine employees. The ability to hire, manage, and train a high-performing AI team will be a sought-after quality, and each of us will need to cultivate many of the same skills that characterize successful entrepreneurs today.

Dennis R. Mortensen[170]

Sometimes when we stop trying to think...when we allow ourselves to observe without intent...that's when the most interesting ideas pop out. That's what happened to Professor Ernesto Gianoli one day in 2014 in a Chilean rainforest.[171] Gianoli is a plant scientist, and most of his time in the field is purposeful and busy with sample collection and cataloguing. That day he put his workload aside, just wandered and observed, and made one of the most intriguing discoveries in the plant world.

He came across a vine he knew called *Boquila trifoliolata* and noticed something peculiar. The vine's leaves had one shape near the forest floor, but when it wrapped itself around a nearby tree its leaves resembled those of the tree. He looked for more *trifoliolata,* and it got even stranger. The vine seemed to mimic the leaves of many other nearby plant species.

Many plants have evolved to mimic the look of other plants. Orchids, for example, are famous mimickers. Except *trifoliolata* was doing more than copying a look of one species from the time of germination. It was showing more fluid abilities by adopting different looks as it grew. It would mimic the leaf size and color too. Sometimes different branches on a single plant would adopt different leaf shapes. No other known plant can mimic a variety of neighbors.[172] *Trifoliolata* is a camouflage expert, but unlike the chameleon, it's doing so without a nervous system.

Although the plant neurobiologists disagree.[173] Yeah...you read that correctly. A small set of researchers, and a larger set of amateur philosophers, believe that plants have a form of nervous system and even aspects of consciousness. Other experts disagree strongly,[174] putting the likelihood that plants have consciousness at "effectively nil."[175]

It has been known for some time that plant motion and direction of growth are sensitive to light. A few species can twist rapidly toward light, and phototropism—the tendency to grow toward light—is a common plant property.

Some plant neurobiologists took that much further. They thought *trifoliolata* plants might have a form of vision—sensing the shape of their neighboring leaves using something like eyes, somehow processing that visual information, and regulating genes and proteins so the plant mimics what it sees. A couple of researchers devised an experiment with *trifoliolata* next to a plastic plant. They claimed the plastic plant's leaf shape was copied by *trifoliolata* [176], but many plant experts chided the experiment as poorly designed.[171] For example, it didn't control for the fact that plants naturally have different leaf shapes at different stages of plant maturity.

There are plenty of other potential explanations. Perhaps chemical scents from nearby plants trigger the change. Maybe microbes or insects carry messages or even genetic material from plant to plant. Genetic influence could be through either epigenetic means (changing the regulation of genes but not the genes itself) or gene transfer (a common phenomenon in microbes). The answer awaits further study.

Aspects of plant neurobiology theories may one day be proven true. I hate to discourage theories...especially counter-cultural ones...because they are an important way to kick thinking out of a rut. This book is intended to do so. However, theories must at some point have evidence, and the plant neurobiology community offers at best circumstantial evidence. For example, neurotransmitter chemicals have been found in plants. However, many common biological chemicals are reused by nature in different ways, and there is no indication those chemicals serve the same function as in an animal nervous system, or even that synapses between plant cells exist.

Why jump to plants having vision—or consciousness? I'm all for provocative theories, but this one feels like wishful thinking. Several responses to criticism say the term "plant neurobiology" is meant as a metaphor.[177] Some of the claims go way beyond metaphor. Not all plant neurobiologists make such claims, but use of the neurobiology term is itself provocative, similar to using the term "intelligence" in describing relatively crude, historical AI.

Plant neurobiology seems a case of anthropomorphism—the tendency to assume human attributes in non-human things. It's a bias that showed up early in human history, and one we may not ever completely shake. Art from the beginning of modern humanity about 40,000 years ago shows anthropomorphic hints of human qualities in animals. Human history also has many examples of anthropomorphism in characterizations of religious deities.

Anthropomorphism isn't limited to interpretations of the natural or supernatural. We also apply human qualities to automation. I worked for a company in the 80s whose warehouse had several robots that shuttled stuff from place to place. The workers had named the robots after Snow White's seven dwarves. Workers seemed firm in the belief that the robots demonstrated their namesakes' personalities.

The anthropomorphic bias is perhaps a logical extension of biases toward other people. As a parent, I commonly misread child thinking and behavior because I ascribed my adult thinking to their immature brains. Along with the rest of humanity, I can find it hard to understand the thinking of those with different backgrounds, cultures, or personalities. Our empathy skills are based on models that are inherently limited by our experiences and imagination. Anthropomorphism seems inevitable—evidently extending as far as plants—because it helps us think about complex, adaptive systems that we don't entirely understand or that we don't have suitable language to describe.

Now we have AI...a non-human entity that can behave in increasingly human ways. How should we think of it? Is it useful to anthropomorphize it? After all, it is automating human work tasks. Or is that dangerous given that AI arrives at its skills via very different mechanisms than do people and makes different kinds of mistakes? Since AI is getting so complicated under the hood, and since AI is increasingly AI-designed and even evolved[178], is there any prayer of understanding it well enough to avoid the human comparison?

One of the key wisdom skills I have glossed over is the ability to select, customize, coordinate, and interpret AI. Workers will be judged by the productivity and effectiveness of themselves and their AI team. Everyone will be a manager, and that means understanding the AI and how it fits in. The way we think about AI is one of the relevant skills.

Managing AI isn't like overseeing prior automations that tend to behave similarly regardless of situation or have predictable failure modes. AI analysis is already so complex...considering information well beyond the ability of our brains...that we won't recognize all the times it messes up.

Managing AI is also about understanding the business objectives, the job priorities, the task breakdown, and even our own strengths and weaknesses. AI is a decision-making tool (including the "decisions" inherent in text generation), and it complements us best when we understand the nuances of our decision making.

Finally, how on earth are we going to keep track of all the AI that I presume will be out there on the market? If there are twenty AI candidates for an audio processing task, then which one should we pick? People can't keep track of all the software tools out there in today's market; that's why we have IT specialists and a technology review industry (that I am never sure whether to trust).

Managing an AI team is then part having an empathy of a sort toward the tech—anthropomorphic or not—part understanding the decision context and the characteristics of the person using the AI, and part product savvy.

Ideally workers will have skills in each of those areas, but let's be realistic. They're going to need help adaptively composing and rejiggering an AI team. My solution is a process called Productivity Therapy.

TECHNOLOGY EMPATHY

We are used to thinking of technology from either a user or a developer point of view. Driving a car (a user) requires motor coordination skills, knowledge of traffic rules and norms, and attention to the way the car is driven (e.g., appropriate speed). In contrast, if someone is building a portion of a car, then every part and fastener has importance. If someone is coding software, so does every line of code. Users and developers have completely different perspectives, and one role doesn't often require deep understanding of the other.

Yet there are perspectives in between users and developers. If my car hiccups when I accelerate at low speed, it's helpful to know about the major functions of the vehicle at a conceptual level. I know acceleration requires fuel and air properly getting into a gas-powered engine, and that that there are air and fuel filters prior to the engine. Maybe my car's hesitation is because one of those filters is clogged?

For thirty-five years Ray and Tom Magliozzi—with the stage names Click and Clack—entertained U.S. audiences on National Public Radio (NPR) with their diagnoses of callers' car woes. They had (and still have via reruns) a much more diverse audience than the topic would imply. People who couldn't care less about car repair would tune in to hear two brothers in thick Boston accents make people smile with their witty banter.

The Car Talk guys were mechanics with enough savvy about cars to predict what went wrong from the context of the ailment. "Nah," they might say, "if the air and fuel filters are clogged that should affect acceleration at all speeds." Alas...my car knowledge is poor enough that I have no idea whether anything in this example is passingly correct.

Click and Clack got their expertise from fixing loads of vehicles. In the process they had to get down to the culprit part or parts. It's a different skill than what's needed for the person who developed that car subsystem. It's also different than the driver knowledge. It's conceptually in between—about how things work in general, how they work together in various use contexts, and what could go wrong.

Understanding technology in those middle-tier abstraction levels is most important in the modern workplace. With those skills you can lead people who use or develop technology even if you've never used or developed. Don't get me wrong; first-hand experience helps, but if people have a Car Talk level of understanding, they are positioned to bridge the developers and users. That's a key part of a manager's job. With the intermediate abstractions they can understand what needs to be developed, or bought, or adapted, because they can map the technology pros and cons to the user level.

I call it technology empathy. It's the skills to use technology in the best ways, to understand wholistically what a technology does, and to anticipate when it will break and how that might manifest. The term empathy is definitely anthropomorphic!

The fictional Mona (the future psychotherapist from Chapter 1) was exhibiting more than tech empathy. She was able to retrospectively assess the evolution of her field. She may have been able to predict how her job would change in the future because of an AI insertion. Those insights require more than technology understanding, but without some tech savvy those judgments would likely be off base.

The nexus between users and developers is where I spent much of my career. Building or selecting an AI capability required examining existing workplaces in detail and imagining what could change because of AI. In my experience, that operational analysis aspect is hard for many AI developers. AI insertion judgments also require understanding whether the technology might be able to do what the operator needs. Few users can help that one.

I was an AI developer for several years. That helps tech empathy. Even though the AI tools are dramatically different from when I did development, the major concepts from my prior experience allow me to quickly understand new AI techniques. I've analyzed many different workplaces in different industries. That also helps tech empathy. I can pick up the new workplace culture or challenge easily because abstract commonalities link them to my prior deep dives.

However, understanding how AI could fit into a workplace requires understanding in both directions: what AI can and can't do, and what will most help a workplace and how. Technology empathy is a multi-factor judgment realm, different from my detailed AI development or industry operations expertise. As discussed in Chapter 3, it deals with a different abstraction level, which in this chapter I can call the Click and Clack level. Technology empathy is more about big-picture wisdom than about detailed expertise.

Ah...but doesn't technology empathy become an expertise? It is a realm with inherent complexity. It requires human judgment with its accompanying values, priorities, problem definitions, goals, expectations, concerns, risks, and trigger points. Under this book's definitions, it is a wisdom realm. The knowledge it relies upon is in the form of heuristics, rules-of-thumb, processes, lessons, and meta-knowledge (knowledge about knowledge).

Technology empathy is the key to human synergy with AI, and we largely don't teach it. What math class have you ever been in that started from a world challenge and asked you to choose the right math for it? No...schools usually teach the other way around. Students are exposed to a bunch of knowledge or methods without the contextual understanding of when to use it.

Let me give an example of how technology empathy comes into play. Imagine that part of Mona's AI team evaluates patient emotional state using the audio and video from online meetings. I'll call the audio and video analyzer "Buddy"—in full-on anthropomorphic style.

In choosing and customizing Buddy, Mona needs to know what it can do well and what it can't. She doesn't need to know the math and code that generates those behaviors. If she knew all the gory details, it likely wouldn't help her decisions because her interest is in the macroscopic AI behaviors. Too much detail could obscure those critical aspects. Similarly, a psychologist doesn't need to know what every neuron in the brain is doing.

Mona also needs to know how Buddy will be used. Would she need answers from the AI in seconds because she wants to use the information as a patient conversation progresses, or would it be OK for the AI to accumulate the information and give a summary at the end of the therapy appointment? Those types of use considerations are prominent in any kind of software selection. The technology must be assessed based on the intended conditions of use.

Yet in many other respects, picking Buddy is quite different from choosing conventional software. AI decision effectiveness could vary because of several situational factors. Perhaps some product candidates don't do well with partial or off-angle views of faces, in low light or sound volume, or when lots of other noise is present. Maybe it messes up when there are data gaps, such as from video or voice freezing for a bit during a telemedicine conversation. Maybe some products have a harder time with some emotions than others and are more uncertain with monotone or stoic faces. It could be that Mona needs simple ways to correct those deficiencies, so the AI doesn't spit out highly uncertain or untrustworthy answers. The number of considerations in selecting an AI product can be enormous.

Am I saying there's no value in understanding the technical methods that AI is using? Perhaps not if the understanding derived from technical depth can be replaced by knowledge at a different abstraction level. You may never need to know how some AI is engineered. You probably should know if the AI is trained on data, what data it used, how its performance was tested, its functional pros and cons, and what those factors could mean for your user experience or its ability to integrate with the rest of the AI team. Most workers will need AI understanding at the Click and Clack level.

There's no reason I can see why games wouldn't be key to growing technology empathy skills. Judgment skills are experientially learned. There are times when it's important to judiciously dig into technology details, but the key skills are processes and lessons for discovering and interpreting knowledge rather than retention of the knowledge itself.

You will never hear this scientist argue for less STEM in schools, but it needs to have a very different orientation. We are avoiding the intermediate level between builder and user. That technology empathy level is the key to AI team management.

SELF-AWARENESS

Way back when...before electricity...I was in graduate school near New York City. A couple of friends and I decided to go to a live, daily talk show—the Phil Donahue Show.

Phil was a character, and for decades he stimulated conversations that were uncomfortable for their time, such as about women's rights and homosexuality. The conversation was intellectual and empathetic, and it intimately involved the audience. Phil would wander around and let audience members ask questions of the guests *du jour*. It was a town hall kind of forum. That day's guests were Denzel

Washington, Jennifer Grey (e.g., *Ferris Bueller's Day Off*, *Dirty Dancing*), and Tom Hulce (e.g., *Amadeus*). They were there to talk about a new made-for-TV movie.

I was fortunate to get a seat on the aisle because I have a bladder the size of a pea. As I sat down in my bright red, cotton, dad sweater (though not yet a dad) I thought "Just listen; you don't need to ask any questions." Nevertheless, halfway through the episode my hand shot up. One of the show assistants spotted me and nodded to Phil that I should be next. Phil wandered over and stopped beside me. At that point, he asked a question of the guests. When they finished, he cocked the long 80's style microphone in my direction with the other arm adopting a kind-of Truman Capote pose that Phil commonly displayed.

I stood up...and completely blanked. I had no idea what the question was going to be, though I did when the hand went up. I grunted "ah, um" into the microphone and got a lucky reprieve. His producer had pointed to another audience member. Phil ran off to get that question, never to return. I'm sure I could have made up a question on the spot. I've had lots of practice with that. I often forget where I am going in mid-sentence.

Those two issues—impulsivity and distractibility—are big ones for me, though well-managed these days. The impulsivity most often showed up in conversation. I might interrupt, ask too many questions, drone on, or complete sentences. The distractibility is harder to describe. On the one hand I can easily get into deep flow states where my mind is completely absorbed in something and notices little else about the world. However, outside of those periods my brain bounces all over the place, including at times I need it to shut down.

I was long aware of the impulsive and distracted behaviors but felt unable to change them. Then I read *Driven to Distraction* about

ADHD (Attention-Deficit/Hyperactivity Disorder).[179] The authors explained the thoughts in patient's heads in various situations...like during conversations. The patients' thoughts echoed my own—amazing but a bit creepy! I decided to get evaluated.

The ADHD stereotypes are a bounce-off-the-walls boy or a daydreamer girl. Those, like all stereotypes, are sometimes inaccurate. I was called hyperactive through most of my childhood. ADHD hadn't yet been invented as a named condition.

ADHD isn't only a childhood condition. There are fundamental differences in how ADHD and non-ADHD brains are wired from birth. ADHD is one of the most heritable of the known mental health conditions.[180] People on the spectrum—a range of ADHD-ness like with autism—can develop various coping mechanisms as an adult, but the condition doesn't go away.

It's also a real thing. I hate that I have to say that, but ADHDs not only have to deal with the condition, but they can be surrounded by those who think it's just an excuse. More kids are diagnosed with ADHD now, and more are given the powerful stimulants that help the condition. Sure...the condition is diagnosed via imperfect means and can be confused with other conditions. Yes...the medications are overprescribed and abused by those who don't need it. Those issues aren't fixed by wishing away the condition.

The statistics are striking. On average ADHDs have a tougher road in life. They make up around 6% of U.S. children (and a lower fraction of adults)[181], but something like a quarter of prisoners[182] and addicts[183]. They are often characterized as screwups because they can't seem to get their act together. Parents and partners wish they'd get organized and stop forgetting their commitments. They can't...to varying degrees...do what others want by willing it. Instead, they need to construct various coping mechanisms to mitigate the impact to their lives.

ADHD happens at a biological level; some of the genes most implicated control things like neuron growth and connection patterns.[184] Most show some improvement as adults with a fully formed frontal lobe and a few coping mechanisms. ADHD can affect learning, but it is not indicative of intelligence.

I got the industry-standard neuropsychiatric tests which examine overall motor, cognitive, and creative skills. It includes a full IQ test. It also had one computer test near the end that gave me fits.

It's a simple test. Single letters appear on a computer screen every few seconds. My job was to push the spacebar on the computer as soon as I could if the letter wasn't a "G" (I just picked that at random; I don't remember the letter that was used). Pretty simple. Push the space bar when not "G."

I stunk at that test. I pushed the space bar most of the time—"G" or not. I lost focus and even forgot the task on occasion. Each time I pushed the space bar when "G" arose, I gave myself a Homer Simpson "Doh!" but I couldn't stop myself. It was a simple test of impulsivity, and I didn't do so well.

I mostly did well on the other tests. My language skills rated a bit better than my analytical skills. That certainly wasn't the case in my SAT days! The tests where I really stood out in a positive way were on the divergent (out-of-the-box) creativity tests.

In one of those, my examiner posed a simple question. "I'm going to give you a letter," she said, "and you have thirty seconds to state as many words as you can that begin with that letter." Those with divergent creativity skills not only list a lot of words, but the pattern of words isn't constrained. They are not simply a list of three letter ones (e.g., sat, sit, set) or ones from one word category (e.g., spider, squirrel, salmon). They are long and short and come from various conceptual categories. I did super on that one.

There are tradeoffs with an ADHD employee (depending of course on the severity and type of the condition and their ability to manage it). They might be impulsive. They could get distracted, go on tangents, or be hard to keep on schedule. On the other hand, they can be important figures for novel perspectives. Evolution may even have favored a few ADHDs in society. They'd be the kind who would be a good scout—attentive to the vibe of the situation, good at adapting, and willing to take risks.

Education about ADHD has been the biggest part of my treatment, and I find that understanding what's going on is very powerful for reshaping intuitive impulsiveness. I'm not defined by ADHD; it's just part of who I am.

Other people will have their own pros and cons. In the AI era, it's important that workers understand themselves and others. Self-awareness factors into selection and management of an AI team.

Managing AI is highly dependent on technology empathy, but it's also a function of us understanding our jobs and tasks. The AI industry and the business community are task focused. However, when AI is democratized—when it can be fit to the needs of individuals—then self-awareness has great currency. For perhaps the first period in history, understanding ourselves has tangible value in the workplace. It can make the difference in whether AI is effectively applied to enhance our performance.

The reasons self-awareness is so important to managing AI is that we each make decisions differently, our decisions are often buried in the unconscious and therefore quite susceptible to emotional or cognitive quirks, and our ability to work efficiently and effectively is subject to different strengths and weaknesses.

For my ADHD, AI could cue me on conversational turn-taking, prompt me to write down thoughts to defuse an impulse, or create a structure that minimizes undirected time where my mind can wander.

The assistance could also combine aspects specific to both my brain's needs and those of the task. For example, in writing this book I found myself yearning for an AI conversation partner. I think better when moving, and I could use AI speech-to-text to transcribe a rough draft of a book section while out for a walk. The problem is that, on my own, my thoughts wander. The transcribed text ends up being so jumbled it's worthless. I stay on point much better if in conversation. The AI conversation partner likely wouldn't need to be too sophisticated. It could behave similarly to a therapist by getting me to dwell on a point longer, ask whether the topic I just talked about is related to that in another transcription, or tell me when I am covering too many topics in too short a time.

The AI community has largely focused on context-independent task assistance. An AI translator doesn't know the context of your request. If the person asking for the translation is an international diplomat, then special care must be taken to ensure it fits the cultural nuances of the intended audience. Human judgment is always needed in deciding how and whether to use automation.

That means we must be savvy to our own judgment influences. We're all deficient in some ways and special in other ways, not only because of varying skill levels, but also because of the underlying way that we think. Improving task performance is dependent on understanding ourselves.

COMPOSING THE AI TEAM

Through the years, I collaborated with many operational communities and had the opportunity to see some commonalities across those boundaries. Workers in many fields would often get different challenges from prior ones, and they would need to quickly analyze the new situation. I saw this most with public health and public safety communities—where every situation was its own unique beast—but it showed up to some degree in nearly every industry I encountered.

Effectively using data analysis to help deal with situational variability is challenged by skill deficits and organizational walls. In the public health infectious disease community, epidemiologists tend not to have much data science or computer programming expertise. There is relevant expertise at public health colleges, and data science gems sprinkled in various public health authorities, but the typical public health authority can't easily leverage those people's skills. The data analysis tools remain in the expert's control, making their bandwidth limit the data analytic capacity for an entire organization and industry. Most often no new information processing can be brought to bear quickly for a new situation.

It is the largest of outbreak challenges that need data analysis the most. Data from small outbreaks can be analyzed manually in many cases. For example, contact tracing—the process of identifying the infectious transmission and pathogen exposure routes—might be possible without software for outbreaks involving tens of people. Automation help is needed for any larger outbreak. Software is required for a volume of contacts even a tiny fraction of the scale of COVID-19.

It would be wise to have data analytics lined up and ready for use in larger-scale situations, but the needs can't be fully anticipated. Data sources are varied and in constant flux. Some sources would emerge because of an outbreak, having no existence beforehand. The pathogens themselves could be novel. Each situation demands different questions and operational collaborators. A flu outbreak that affects mainly the elderly might need data sharing with senior care facilities, while one that has a great impact on children would value data from childcare centers.

Unanticipated situations require new ways of looking at data, but even software-skilled analysts can't do work instantly. Data analysts often must try many techniques or visualizations to find ones that work best for the problem. New challenges require swift action and reengineering a data processing pipeline isn't swift.

The combination of scarce skill resources, significant situational variation, and urgent needs called for a new solution. I enlisted one of my best software developers to design an environment where new or augmented data processing chains could be rapidly assembled to suit the problem *du jour*. We called the resulting capability Composable Analytics.[185]

Epidemiology was the application that guided our design, but the challenges are common to many jobs in an information-powered workplace. A worker often needs to analyze something quickly, and there's no time to start from scratch. The key is to find existing pieces that can be tweaked or stitched together. Workers may know the guru elsewhere in the company but can't access their time. Then the data analysis is often abandoned, or some quick but more cursory analysis is performed instead.

Composable analytics had several key elements. At its core, the platform allowed pre-existing modules to be tweaked by dragging and dropping them visually into new combinations and by exposing control knobs, so users don't have to dig into the code. Quickly creating a data processing flow in this way doesn't require software programming skill *per se*, but it does require technology empathy to make sure the modules are being used in appropriate ways. We imagined that those with some data processing expertise would be responsible for the module composition. Eventually, most workers will need to be able to do some form of AI team coordination and adaptation.

A second key Composable Analytics feature was having a repository of processing modules ready for use. The modules needed a few important features. Trust is critical whenever details are hidden from view. Modules added to the environment were attributed to specific creators. The community knows the data processing experts. Moreover, the lineage of the software was visible and attached to the processing outputs.

An important characteristic of the environment was the ability to have modules at varying levels of abstraction. A software module could be as simple as adding two numbers, or it could be an extremely complex AI. Multi-module compositions could be stored as a single module for future use in other processing pipelines. This kept the complexity of processing chains manageable for human brains.

Finally, the results of processing data could be shared with other organizations or individuals in a single environment, replacing ad hoc sharing through point-to-point channels.

Productivity therapy requires technology empathy and self-awareness in addition to problem and task understanding. It also needs a way to quickly bring AI and software to bear on a new challenge. Composable Analytics exemplifies characteristics of future AI team management platforms: the ability to leverage those with strong technology skill, the ability to quickly create or modify a new team, and a way to learn from others' experiences with their AI teammates.

CHANGE MANAGEMENT VIA AN AGILE PROCESS

In the 80s and 90s the business world began migrating toward a different paradigm for constructing and managing complex systems. In manufacturing, inventory management, and logistics, the notion of a static design gave way to continuous improvement processes made up of lots of little steps.

In software development, the traditional "waterfall" process—where the requirements and design of a product are developed up front and stay unchanged—was replaced by various forms of Agile development (capitalized because it refers to a defined change process rather than the colloquial meaning of the word). In Agile, the goals and design are iteratively developed.[186]

These changes weren't fads. They were responses to a complex world with plenty of uncertainty. A logistics pipeline could be disrupted through no fault of the company; we've seen that impact with the COVID-19 pandemic. Smaller changes in a global economy mean plans must be adjusted frequently. Similarly, a multi-year software development process could go off the rails if the objectives were wrong. Perhaps what users wanted wasn't well understood after all, or the market or competition for the software might change during development.

Agile software development is now the standard, and it is a far more successful process than the all-up-front waterfall method in terms of cost, timeline, and project failure rates.[187] The ability to morph quickly and have a usable solution as soon as possible is the logical solution to change and uncertainty that cannot be controlled.

Adoption of Agile in the software community took decades. It is fought by more traditional business thinking that insists on all the answers being presented up front. Agile is implicitly admitting limitations in everyone's crystal ball. People can't know all the conditions the solution will have to face. Assumptions may no longer be valid. Users often change their mind on what they want when they use software versus imagine using it. It has taken the past couple of decades to build the evidence showing that Agile is a superior method compared to a sequential design-build-test process.

Agile processes aren't just for software. In principle they are necessary whenever a system is very complex—either the one being built or the one that a product is affecting. Complexity means the ramifications of choices can be unclear, a bunch of the system is uncontrollable, and the goal posts may have to move.

Agile processes vary in the particulars, but typically they break up development into small time chunks called Sprints. Each Sprint defines tasks and goals for that period, with frequent but brief coordination during it. The goals for each Sprint are debated at the beginning, and tasks are assigned based on the long-term vision and stakeholder reaction to a working implementation from the prior Sprint period.

There are at least four critical elements of an Agile process:

- The assumption of frequent and incremental change.
- A requirement to build a usable product at each step. In other words, don't just think—do—and do in a way that the outcome can be experientially evaluated.
- The empowerment of all stakeholders in the process, especially the customers (as more than window dressing).
- The expectation of a solution-oriented team that will measure progress frequently and jettison what is not working.

Agile has completely changed the mentality of the software world. When Silicon Valley talks about failing fast and often on the path to innovation, they are extrapolating an Agile product development process to business management and venture capital investment.

If workers are to become capable of the continuous change that the world demands, not only must they have the will and skills to change, but they must also have the expectation of change. Agile-like processes enforce that expectation. Change is a habit too.

§

When each worker is measured by what they and their AI team produce, then everyone is a manager.

I don't expect everyone to use AI tools effectively or properly on their own. They will need help, and Productivity Therapy is my solution to that quandary. I imagine a literal counseling process, where an expert will discuss job, task, and individual decision needs, suggest products and customizations, share best practices, and aggregate individual needs into company ones. These therapists would be the Click and Clack of organizations, although working with minds and AI instead of cars and wrenches.

It would be great if every user could understand what AI modules do so they can anticipate when they are providing reliable answers. However, AIs are giant black boxes of such complexity that even the developers don't understand all the gotchas. That understanding will come from a distributed set of people who tickle the AI in different ways.

Let's imagine that we can make people 10% more productive with the right AI (or software) tools. I argue that most of our work will be accomplished by machines in the future, but I'll keep the percentage small anyway. That means one productivity therapist could pay for themself if serving only ten other people.

Companies don't need to wait until AI's transformation is in full bloom. Productivity therapy can happen now. Software tools are already not being leveraged to improve workers to the degree that they could be.

Just don't expect that IT departments will necessarily be the Productivity Therapists. Not only don't IT experts typically have AI expertise, but they are not necessarily business, task, or psychology experts either. As this chapter has explained, each of those talents is necessary. A software tool that helps workers in one way can easily be counter-productive at other times.

I began this chapter by asking whether we can think of AI "workers" anthropomorphically. The most precise answer is no. AI may appear to be making decisions like people, but it isn't. AI is both better and worse at tasks than people, depending on their design, training set, quality control, and context of use. Still...I think anthropomorphism is inevitable. We will consider them people-ish anyway. Their output is increasingly indistinguishable from that of people, and it's in our nature to anthropomorphize.

I'm not sure that's a bad thing. Worker teammates can also be black boxes. They each make different mistakes and uniquely react to situations. They are even different workers from one day to the next, including according to whether they slept well. At least an AI doesn't show that variation.

Go ahead and think of AI in human ways, but with the under-stand-ing that these savant-like "creatures" don't really know the big picture. That's our job.

The last chapter suggests ways to move education toward wisdom.

9.

INSTRUMENTS OF CHANGE

You keep plugging away – that's the way social change takes place. That's the way every social change in history has taken place: by a lot of people, who nobody has ever heard of, doing work.

Noam Chomsky[188]

New York City has the largest public school system in the U.S. with over 1,800 schools and one million students. In 2009, one of those schools tried something very different. The Quest to Learn (Q2L) school that serves 6th through 12th graders was designed around game design and play. It is still going strong.[189]

Student engagement was the primary motivation. One report from that time showed around half of high school students in the U.S. were disengaged from school.[190]

At the same time, the growing focus on 21st-Century Skills was motivating a school model that emphasizes skills such as creativity, teamwork, and critical thinking. Q2L teaches the same curriculum as the state mandates but tries to do so through play constructs.

Q2L emphasizes seven principles:[191]

- "Everyone is a participant;
- Challenge is constant;
- Learning happens by doing;
- Feedback is immediate and ongoing;

- Failure is reframed as 'iteration';
- Everything is interconnected; and
- It kind of feels like play."

These principles manifest in different ways depending on the learning goal, as described in Jordan Shapiro's 2014 article.[192] Students in English class play Socratic Smackdown to teach argumentation skills. Rock-onimoes is a version of dominos that addresses geology concepts. Students are often helping improve the game in addition to learning from it.

Researchers were funded to analyze the impact of the Q2L paradigm. In one analysis, students were assessed using the College and Work Readiness Assessment (CWRA+). The CWRA+ tries to measure scientific and numerical reasoning, problem solving, and writing effectiveness that are big parts of critical thinking. The average student improvement at Q2L over one year of middle school on the CWRA+ was comparable to four years of growth of a college student on a similar test. Importantly, English language assessments and attitudes toward school also improved.[189]

Q2L showed these gains without cherry-picking the student population. Two-thirds of the students are from low-income families, and nearly a third have special needs.[193] Despite that, Q2L was in the top 20% of all New York City schools for math and reading proficiency in 2021.[194]

Great—Q2L is on to something! The bad news is that the school was started fifteen years ago. Why don't we see the paradigm spreading all over the place?

To be clear, Q2L has aspects of the paradigm I'm espousing (the game part) but is still addressing a conventional curriculum. But Q2L is only meant as an example of a vanguard school. There are several others sprinkled around the country...like some that have adopted the Challenge-Based Learning paradigm I described earlier. There are a few colleges like Northeastern University that emphasize experiential learning. The learning and engagement outcomes from these models are good. Why haven't the models spread?

One of the simple answers is that it takes resources to transform. Q2L has a dedicated team that helps teachers incorporate game aspects into their teaching, and the school was built using funding from a sizable grant.

Cost is a frequent roadblock in many transformations, but there's more to it than that. The educational system is not inherently adaptable. This final chapter asks why, and what can be done about it.

A wisdom pivot is a daunting challenge because of the speed of AI's advance. How can it blossom quickly? This question deserves way more than a chapter, but I'll get the conversation started.

If there is a baked-in system, then external incentives must be applied. If you try to turn around a big ship quickly then you need help from outside the ship. You need tugboats. The three tugboats I want to highlight are: the skill demand signals from business; accountability measurements and associated curriculum standards in education; and...where possible...competitive pressures and rewards to improve schools and teaching.

BUSINESS' DEMAND SIGNALS

It is one of the most glaring of business deficiencies, and it's not isolated to one sector, or culture, or personality. In hiring the best workers, we're getting it all wrong. The typical process of posting a job opening, screening resumes, and conducting unstructured interviews has little power to predict future job performance.[195] Yet that's how most hiring gets done. Industries exist that perpetuate that model. It doesn't work.

This discussion of hiring may seem tangential, but the educational system needs a clear demand signal from business. Those communities do not have enough connection. Business makes general claims that they aren't getting enough workers with strong 21st-Century Skills, but they don't have the measurements to show it. Without that data, they cannot provide a clear feedback signal that is a target of improvement for colleges (at a minimum).

It's a bit perplexing why hiring practices haven't advanced further given the importance of having the right human capital. Perhaps companies just don't want to be the outlier. It's always hard to get leadership to adopt something atypical. Leaders are judicious about sticking their necks out if they do it at all. Maybe the efficiency allure of AI resume screening is overruling what human resource departments know is best. For sure, people overrate their ability to judge other people without significant bias. We are drawn to those like us or can become captive to great talkers or lying (yes...interviewees routinely lie). We think we can see through the answers to some greater insight on the person. Studies show that isn't true; such interviews can reveal more about the interviewer than the job candidate.[195]

It wasn't always this way. It is relatively recently that resumes (from the French word meaning "to summarize") became a required element of a job search. Its first use is unclear, but some attribute it to Leonardo da Vinci who in 1482 penned a letter to the Duke of Milan that listed his prior work and skills. Today we might call that a cover letter. By 1950, having a resume was a required step in a hiring process.[196]

Today, resumes are a required step in hiring unless one's professional network can sidestep it. There's no reason to believe that wisdom skills can be gleaned from a resume even if the candidate has highlighted them. Automated resume screening systems focus on keywords and phrases, thereby incentivizing buzz word loading of resumes that often exaggerate abilities. I would have this conversation often with contracting shop representatives. They wanted to know what buzz words to look for; I wanted to find the best thinkers. We weren't talking the same language.

It's hard to understand the relevance of a resume for assessing wisdom skills. We know GPA doesn't capture those intangibles well, and besides, GPA is a weak predictor of job performance.[197,198] Resumes are essential since some summary of yourself is needed, but screening resumes isn't the best way to find candidates with industry-spanning wisdom qualities. I assume that some of the better candidates never make it to the interview stage.

Ah...but then interviewing will be more revealing...right? Isn't that when an organization really gets to see what people are made of, and whether they know their stuff?

Nah—interviewing has problems too. The most common sort of interview is unstructured. It consists of an informal conversation with the candidate. Many analyses show unstructured interviews are only slightly better than flipping a coin.[199] Worse yet, they are probably harmful given the numerous biases humans are known to have regarding personality, the ability to detect deception, physical appearance, etc.[200] Unstructured interviews are one example of when we don't want gut feel to rule our decisions. Unfortunately, hiring managers incorrectly think they're better at it than others.[201]

Structured interviews add more rigor to the process by ensuring that all candidates are asked the same questions and judged against the same criteria. This has been shown to reduce human biases relative to unstructured interviews and be a better predictor of job performance.[202] However, a big grain of salt should be added to such interpretations. Interviewers' biases remain. Things such as applicant appearance, and nonverbal cues like smiling, tone, pitch and speech rate, are shown to impact interview ratings. Structured interviews may reduce, but not eliminate, those biases. Candidates may try to game the process and adopt a style and answers that may not be reflective of their typical behaviors and attitudes. As more personality testing is used in the hiring process, organizational biases could creep in.

Maybe those brainteaser questions are more useful, like the ones Google became known for? For example, a candidate might be asked "If you were shrunk to the size of a pencil and put in a blender, how would you get out?" The supposed intent is to understand how people think through a problem. Google analyzed the data about its hiring process and learned as early as 2013 that the brain teasers don't work.[203] Candidate responses to teasers did not predict future performance. One purpose of the brain teasers was to see how well somebody could think on their feet, but how often does a computer programmer have to do that? Their job allows thinking through a challenge without social pressure or a timer.

There is a better way. Applicants can be evaluated based on what they can do rather than what they say about themselves. The best predictor of future job performance is general mental ability.[197] There is some indication that employers understand this, at least implicitly. More companies now require college degrees for jobs that historically didn't need them (e.g., administrative roles). Perhaps they're using the presence of a degree as a proxy for mental skills. If so, then maybe they shouldn't; the evidence shows they're better off measuring cognitive ability directly.[204]

IQ scores are well correlated with future performance, though calling anything an IQ test in a hiring process is downright dangerous because of discriminatory uses in the past. However, measurements of skills like verbal reasoning, logic, and numeric ability (as examples) are more predictive than GPA, interviews, or education level.

There is plenty of incentive for the business community to provide better wisdom competency measures. Hiring is an expensive process, especially if the hire fails. Showing shortfalls in critical thinking, communication, problem solving, or other wisdom skills can begin to create a scorecard against which schools can adapt in a competitive higher-education environment. I can imagine resumes that list scores on validated cognitive tests versus other less predictive measures in today's resumes.

Of course, businesses have job-specific skill needs too. The second-best predictor of job performance is job tryout. Hello internships and apprenticeships![197] Those are impractical for many job openings, so a proxy tends to be the performance on knowledge tests (e.g., legal bar exam).

Thomas Edison may have been one of the first to use such pre-hire testing at scale. He introduced a 140+ question quiz to screen his applicants. It wasn't like you'd imagine a modern job quiz that might examine personality or industry understanding. It was more like Jeopardy with questions about facts unrelated to work tasks, like "Who reached the South pole?" and "Where is Copenhagen?"[205]

Games are the way to go for testing wisdom rather than knowledge. A few employers are catching on. Google's Foobar Challenge[206] is the name given to a computer programming challenge presented in pseudo-game form (pseudo-game because it may not provide feedback on the level of success; that aspect is unclear). The player develops computer programs to address challenges over five difficulty levels in a fictional outer-space scenario. Google gets to see how candidates think and work.

It's important for me to distinguish between gamification and gaming. Gamification is a form of incentivization for otherwise non-game processes. For example, Deloitte's Badgeville built rewards into its otherwise conventional leadership learning platform.[207] Hackathon competitions are used as hiring tools for computer scientists.[208] Those aren't games, but they borrow features from them.

Other games are used to generate interest in a profession, but it's not clear that the tasks within those games map directly to the skills needed for a job. For example, the U.S. Air Force's game Airman Challenge tries to show how Air Force careers are both interesting and important.[209] However, there is an unclear mapping from the skills needed in the game to the skills needed in a particular job role in the Air Force.

A small number of companies use games as part of hiring processes. Telekom—the largest telecommunications company in Hungary—used a game instead of resume screening to recruit new salespeople in 2018.[210] The games they used analyzed competencies like problem-solving skill and endurance that were associated with their best performers. Some of the candidates they hired were previously rejected by resume screening. Those hired using the games quickly reached the performance levels of strong performers.

Games in interview processes can examine skills that are beyond an expertise like computer programming. The technology exists to examine intangible qualities too, such as communication, teamwork, and interpersonal dynamics.

I want colleges and students to be able to use the same games (appropriately varied to avoid "teaching to the test") to evaluate how well prepared they are for particular careers. That will require industry or professional societies to step up and help coalesce or define the general cognitive abilities and skill demonstrations that are needed for specific job types. The point is to be able to evaluate how well workers are prepared for various roles, thereby exerting an accountability signal from the macro-customer of the education system (a student being the micro-customer).

Maybe the resume buzz words of the future can be candidate scores and progression levels on 21st-Century and job-relevant games.

EDUCATION STANDARDS AND ACCOUNTABILITY

Testing has been present in various forms throughout American educational history.[211] The Progressive education movement gained prominence around the 1940s, and with that philosophy came a focus on applying scientific methods to education. That required understanding results. Most of the early standardized tests were locally designed and administered. The exception was for college entry where The College Boards created national exams for U.S. college admission processes beginning in the early 20th century.

Other than for college entrance, there was little accountability for student performance on either students or schools. The practice of social promotion recognized the potential harm of separating students from their age cohorts, so schools promoted children to the next grade regardless of test scores.

The Coleman report in 1966 is recognized as the beginning of a bigger focus on accountability.[212] It examined how resources and opportunities are different for students of different races, but it focused on results and engendered conversations about structural problems in education.

Education was the top expenditure for every state by the 80s, and officials wanted to rein it in. There was tension between educators who wanted more resources and public officials who wanted to see results. That tension exists to this day.

The signature K-12 federal education reforms of the 21st-century—*No Child Left Behind* and *The Every Student Succeeds Act*—emphasized standardized tests and curriculum (termed the Common Core) for English language and math (and later, for science). There has been backlash from many quarters. Some states balked at more federal control. Schools didn't like the accountability teeth in the legislation that put a target on schools that weren't getting good scores. Educators worried about "teaching to the test"—reducing the emphasis on subjects that aren't tested. Schools with a higher fraction of English language learners or special-needs students thought they were being punished for factors out of their control.

The test scores did improve for a while. High school graduation rates increased. Math scores steadily increased in the 00s but have leveled off since.[213] The possible impact of a constriction in curricular offerings has evidence on both sides, but over the long-term students are completing more required years of study in subjects beyond math and English than they did decades ago.[214]

National and state standards, tests, and accountability are now baked into the social and political conversation. They are likely here to stay. Top-down pressure on schools will always be fought to some degree, but it's important to recognize that they are one of the few tools available to avoid an educational Wild West. The question isn't whether to have these tools; it's what the tools should be trying to do.

We need to face a few basic facts. Despite spending a lot more on schools (more on that a bit later) and emphasizing results, the improvements have been on the margins. In 2019, only a third of high school seniors in the U.S. were at a level considered proficient in reading and only a fourth were in math.[215] We're beating our heads against an unyielding wall. Are we at the limits of what the existing school model can achieve?

Rather than using standards, testing, and accountability to reinforce the existing knowledge-oriented paradigm, we should be using it as a tool for change. The focus of testing and accountability should be the less frequently taught subjects that are crucial for the modern age. We should be measuring schools by how well they can adapt, not by how well they can teach an already outdated paradigm.

I know innovation-oriented states and schools are already thinking about new types of tests and standards that will give a glimpse of 21st-Century Skill competencies. I have put one form of assessment on the table (games) that could create powerful feedback to innovators at the local level about wisdom skills. There's no reason a student can't be explicitly tested on critical thinking, interpersonal relations, and other aspects considered intangible and untestable.

It's time we use standards and accountability to create change, not lock in the status quo.

TEACHERS

Let's say there is progress in getting measurable, wisdom-related skill demand signals from businesses. Moreover, assume curriculum standards and assessments focus more on wisdom skills, and schools and teachers are rewarded for innovation. If the incentives line up correctly, then teachers and administrators will finally get the freedom to innovate, and the direction of innovation would be pointed toward wisdom.

What then? Would teachers and administrators be able to adapt?

Undoubtedly, resources would be needed for the change. As the Quest to Learn model shows, specialists of a sort that are not typical in education were needed to help teachers get to the new model.[216] Change tends to increase cost and stress for a while. That's the way it goes; as with changes that other workers experience, it will pull educators out of their comfort zones.

Teacher preparation in college will need a dramatic reshaping, but I won't focus on that because it is the slow way to change the system, and AI's progress demands urgency. Only 13% of the 4+ million K-12 teachers in the U.S. are under the age of thirty.[217] The reality is that change will need to come from the existing teacher talent pool.

Let me start from what we know about great teaching. There is little doubt, either from our personal experiences or from educational research, that teachers have a tremendous effect on student achievement. The effect of great teaching has a larger effect than that of better schools.[218]

Ideally, teachers should have some wisdom themselves. It isn't necessary that teachers be at a professorial level in critical thinking, communication, or another wisdom topic. Wisdom for an elementary school student can look a lot like common sense to adults. Rather, the transition to a wisdom paradigm will require a lot of tradeoffs and innovations. The change requires wisdom. The question is whether teachers already have those qualities.

We are missing a lot of information about teacher wisdom as with other professions. Such measures are used infrequently and are highly imperfect. As the last section discussed, general cognitive abilities are shown to be great predictors of job performance across a wide range of professions. The impact is higher for more complex professions that typically require more education, but the positive effect is seen in clerical workers, drivers, managers, typists, police officers, and clerks.[219] It seems to be a general principle. The good news is that the median K-12 teacher IQ is above average, with college professors rating near the top of all professions. Much of what teachers must be good at won't show up strongly on an IQ test, but it's the data we have.

However, for some reason general cognitive skills don't seem to help teacher performance. A range of studies—some looking at aspects of general intelligence, and some at proxies for it (e.g., college entrance exam scores that are correlated with general cognitive skill)—show little effect on teaching performance.[220] That's true whether teaching effectiveness is based on administration ratings of teachers or on student achievement.

Why would better teacher general cognitive abilities not matter? That isn't clear. There could be methodological problems in the studies, or some difference in dealing with children versus adults. Maybe the most important teacher skills aren't well represented in the test content...but wouldn't that be true for other professions as well?

Other aspects of teacher training and abilities are just as puzzling. Many K-12 schools in the U.S. require that teachers eventually get a master's degree, and almost all pay more for teachers with graduate degrees. Getting an extra degree can be a hardship for teachers. They add to an already busy schedule and low pay with extra coursework and expense over several years. It must be important...right? Evidently not. Getting a master's degree does not statistically lead to better teaching.[221]

What does matter is teaching experience.[221] That implies that there is wisdom in being a great teacher which, like for other fields, is difficult to capture in available data. "Duh," says every teacher reading this. I speculate that the key aspects of that wisdom relate to understanding student needs, maintaining a good learning environment in the classroom, getting kids engaged, and time management that keeps the teacher organized across many responsibilities. Those should transfer to a very different paradigm.

The change in the content and the tools for teaching wisdom skills may not transfer as easily to a new model. There is no reason to believe that a teacher will be great at understanding or solving big real-world challenges across many domains. They don't get the practice doing so.

There are a few ways to deal with that inexperience.

One is to accept that the teacher shouldn't be expected to be all-knowing about what they teach. Rather, the teacher should facilitate a process for figuring things out, with both teacher and student learning as they go. There is evidence that is best for both teachers and students. As John Hattie said in his book *Visible Learning*, "The remarkable feature of the evidence is that the biggest effects on student learning occur when teachers become learners of their own teaching, and when students become their own teachers."[218]

The problem-solving inexperience does require technological help. It means having real-world challenges teed up by those who are the gurus. It means having ways to deliver experiences at the heart of learning wisdom. Those canned experiences must come through game and lesson libraries. AI tutors could get both teachers and students unstuck or provide detailed information when the problem requires it.

Educators are used to thinking about education technology as conventional IT, help with education administration, devices like smart boards, or robots in the occasional computer science class. That's all the education market requires right now for the knowledge-first delivery model. A wisdom-first model is different though since breadth of understanding is emphasized over depth of knowledge. That makes it harder for any one person to know what knowledge will be needed and prepare for it.

One of the absolute keys to enabling teacher and school transition is empowering the education technology industry to creatively support a very different kind of curriculum. Right now, there are only small, specialized markets for those companies if they can't fit their product into the existing knowledge-delivery paradigm.

Finally, there is the issue of teacher incentives. Change requires more energy than the status quo, but teachers are not monetarily rewarded for better teaching or extra effort. Most school districts base teacher pay solely on years of service and degree level. There is no tangible incentive for excellence. Fortunately, teachers are a very caring and passionate crowd. They want to do better for their students, and many go above and beyond the minimum responsibilities.

Yet what I'm advocating is massive change. Top-down changes can chart the course, but only empowerment of local schools and staff will move the ship. It is through lots of experimentation, coalescence of lessons and best practices, and encouragement from the public and government that major progress will be made. Teachers and administrators need more than encouragement; they need rewards.

There is much consternation in the teaching community about their pay level, and with good cause. American teachers are near the bottom of the international pack in how much they are paid relative to similarly educated workers.[222] High school teachers would have to be paid 20-80% higher to reach the same relative pay level as in most European countries.

It's not because the U.S. isn't investing in education. The average inflation-adjusted spending per public school student increased 400% from 1960 to 2019.[223] Most of that—around 80% as of 2017—goes to staffing costs.[224] Yet teacher salaries haven't increased. Average, inflation-adjusted teacher salaries are essentially flat since 1990, and even a bit down since the 2008 recession.[225] The reason for the apparent contradiction is that the number of teachers and support personnel is dramatically higher—almost doubling from 1970 to 2012—despite a roughly level number of students.[226] This arose both because of a push to reduce class sizes, thereby increasing the number of classroom teachers, and an even larger increase in non-teaching staff.[226]

That cannot continue. More teachers aren't the answer; better ones are, and money incentives are needed to get better ones. We need enticements for our brightest to join the teaching corps and rewards for better performance. Without that, major change in education might be stunted regardless of top-down pressures.

COMPETITION

As much as I'd like to avoid the politically polarizing topic of school competition, it is hard for me to believe that a necessary level of innovation will occur without aspects of a free market that rewards innovative teachers and schools.

One cannot get very far into current education debates without being exposed to the one about competition between schools, usually expressed in the language of school choice or vouchers. The debate is starkly drawn on the two political sides, but deep-thinking people know that both points of view have merit.

The pro school-choice crowd wants families to have control over how the education money used for their student is spent. They want parents to decide on the school. There is no question that competition has value. It is a fundamental of a market-based system and is shown to improve products and services.

The other side sees danger from vouchers or related constructs. They see market systems as amplifiers of inequality, and there is plenty of evidence for that too. Completely free markets are likely to benefit great schools that are predominantly in wealthier communities. The local neighborhood school in a disadvantaged area could get even worse, especially if the better schools select students based on merit or cost (e.g., not taking special needs students). The local school is an important pillar of communities, and loss of schools in poorer areas could only exacerbate neighborhood woes.

I don't have answers to this debate, but the grounds for compromise are evident. Each side makes important points. The status quo isn't working. The Wild West won't either. There is plenty of room in the middle for innovative approaches.

One of the advantages of the decentralized American educational system is that variation of approach should improve best practices over time. That is critical because education is a complex system, and even the most informed and logical approaches will have unintended consequences. "Leverage points frequently are not intuitive," says systems expert Donella Meadows, "Or if they are, we too often use them backward, systematically worsening whatever problems we are trying to solve."[227] Big national or state-wide changes are giant gambles if they are overly prescriptive. We can easily get it wrong, creating unintended consequences that push the system in the wrong direction. Those top-down pressures need to encourage local innovation and propagation of lessons, not detailed mandates.

Local innovation could also be fed by student and parent choice. Right now, the only ones that get choice (excepting college) are those who can afford to send their children to a private school or to home school. Wealth will always confer advantages, but it is the socioeconomically disadvantaged that are the biggest future economic opportunity. When we can bring them in as full members of the economy then they buy products and services. They use fewer government services. They become economic accelerants and we become a healthier society.

It's time for each side to stop being absolutist or use inflammatory rhetoric. There is a lot of room for great solutions.

§

This book is intended to start a conversation, but we're running out of time. AI is accelerating downhill, and at best we're standing to the side going "hey...look at that."

I am all for addressing the many potential dangers that AI advancement could bring. They are complex and daunting.

How humanity evolves is at least as important. If we cannot step up and provide the wisdom that complements AI, then technology might consume those roles too. If human judgment is a coin flip, then machines could do the flipping. Too many of us will end up on the discard pile competing for low-wage work.

It will take brave leaders, innovative thinkers, and intelligent incentivization of market forces to get us where we need to go as quickly as we need to get there. I think we can do it.

If we do it's because society gets mobilized, not just schools. The change also needs business and worker-group leadership. It needs authorities to make wise choices. The change needs us—workers, parents, educators, and our individual threads of the societal tapestry. We each have a role. This must be a movement, and movements work best when they're addressed from many angles.

"We'll figure it out," you may say. "We continue to prosper because the free market works out the kinks." I have zero sympathy for a laissez-faire attitude. Somehow the same people saying we should take a hands-off view at the societal level would never say a company should behave similarly.

There are inklings of hope. Some businesses are figuring out that there are better ways to hire and develop talent that fits the modern world. There are vanguard schools that demonstrate elements of what I am proposing. Many people express concerns about work, school, and tunnel vision thinking. In their own ways, they are addressing the central challenge of this book—that the old ways of doing things aren't going to work anymore. However, each of these encouraging signals are tiny relative to this issue's importance.

The current path won't get us where we need to go. It clearly hasn't. Business has wanted different and improved workers for decades, including not only more technically trained ones, but also those with 21st-Century Skills. The desire hasn't percolated into major change.

Education isn't capitalistic. Oh...sure...colleges compete, but unlike with business, we can't measure success by revenue and profit. There is poor understanding of which colleges produce more successful students (in the long-term of a career), and what about the school or its population engendered that success. As for K-12 education, the system is distributed in terms of responsibility, but with at best weakly competitive aspects that push evolution.

Monumental change is resisted at every turn. There seems to be little we can agree upon. Our minds look backward more than forward. The plight of the disadvantaged tugs at empathetic hearts but isn't as tangible as the struggles in our own microcosms.

The wisdom pivot can't be a typical movement where progress is measured on generational scales. Like with climate change, there is a deadline—albeit with a gray boundary.

Curbing the advancement of AI has little hope of working in the near-term. I am all for international agreements that, for example, might keep us from becoming even more efficient war makers, but there are disincentives galore. There is simply too much money in AI, too much power up for grabs, and too much scientific curiosity. The genie is out of the bottle, and I don't know how we can put it back in. Plus, AI is critical in helping us address super-complex problems that are beyond what our brains can handle. We need the help even as we fear it.

I could advocate for extensive and forceful top-down mandates. That might work for authoritarian regimes, but it doesn't work in the U.S. I don't think that is the best path anyway. Too much control stifles innovation, and surely a wisdom rebalancing needs plenty of creative minds. Nobody has all the answers.

Please join me. Tell me where I'm wrong. Let's get the conversation going. One step at a time moves us forward. If enough of us are stepping, then we can make it happen.

EPILOGUE AND ACKNOWLEDGMENTS

Wisdom Factories didn't emerge in response to the latest AI developments. It was brewing since at least 2018, and it is far more than a book to me. It's representative of years of personal and professional transformation and is as much a fulfillment of my psychological needs as it is a societal call to action.

The initial impetus was simply to communicate in a different way.

Whether in pitching a new idea or in describing project results, I often felt my most important points—the ones that placed the work in a broader motivational and impact context—were precisely the ones that listeners didn't absorb. That strongly impacted how transformative I could be.

For example, getting funding for game development was a slog for many years. Some seemed to look at it as a nice-to-have way to get people engaged in thinking through some issue; I saw it as a critical step in understanding the decisions that technology needs to support. To them, games were demos; to me, they were science. Some confused them with frivolous entertainment games, decried the qualitative nature of some of the gaming lessons, or in other ways expressed disdain. They seemed to worry that games could even disturb their image as serious scientists.

I never expect to convince everyone, and I too was dubious about gaming when a few of my most creative coworkers came to me with their initial idea many moons ago. Yet some decision makers saw the value right away. It got to the point where we could tell immediately whether an audience would be receptive to gaming as a scientific or educational tool; the presenter's chief comment after a briefing was on whether the decision maker "got it"...in a big-picture sense. Years after we began game-related work, many moved to the "got it" side, but others never did. A few remained downright hostile to it.

In a strangely intertwined way, I ended up writing a book about building games to better teach how to deal with AI development because I was thinking about why I couldn't teach about games that would help develop AI. (Don't bother trying to reread that! It won't make more sense the second time.)

I talked to mentors about this issue. "You're a couple of steps ahead of others' thinking," I was told. "Their brains aren't ready for it," another said.

Those answers, while perhaps true, were unsatisfactory. I was likely behind others' thinking at other times. What was it about brains that "get it" that distinguishes them, at least for that moment, from those that don't?

I wondered whether there was something we could do better with our argument or approach to such conversations. I knew that all the briefing slides in the world wouldn't carry a brain over that hump, but playing a game might, or communicating differently could.

I thought perhaps there were two problems in my communication style: a briefing didn't allow enough immersion in the topic for the big picture to sink in, and I was providing a dry, logical explanation when a storytelling form would be more impactful.

I turned to writing, but that exposed a major deficiency—I wasn't a good writer. I didn't have any experience writing in a less dense, narrative form for more general audiences. I wasn't asked to write much in high school, and I received no writing instruction through four years of undergraduate and five years of graduate study. There were few who helped my writing during thirty years of work (with a notable exception...thank you Beth Ducot!). My on-the-job writing practice was limited to dense technical articles.

So the writing stunk for quite a while. I am very appreciative of the few people who were willing to read my early musings. I feel they deserve an apology! Very slowly my voice emerged, though I am still in a steep part of the learning curve.

For those of you with the *chutzpah* to try something very new, keep telling yourself you can do it. If it's important enough to you, then it'll click at some point.

I had been thinking about and working on this book topic for years without getting very far. Suddenly it fell into place. The first draft came together in six weeks in late 2022 and early 2023. It used little of my prior writing and didn't need major overhauls in subsequent drafts (though you readers might disagree?). My voice and my story finally came together.

That it took so long was as much a function of the limits of my intuition and the nature of my brain as it was my writing inexperience. I feel big-picture insights more so than I think them. It takes time to interrogate that intuition and create a logical explanation for it. That process in turn changes the nature of the intuition, giving it more nuance or at times forcing a realization that the gut wasn't right that time.

By the time the book crystalized, I felt the writing process helped more than to improve my explanatory powers. It helped me think better in the moment, and that also changed the nature of my interpersonal interactions. I realized that my penchant for asking lots of questions or droning on wasn't only a tendency of my ADHD; it was also because I had a yearning to get my acquired insights out of my head. There was ego in this for sure, but less so than it may have appeared from the outside. I had another internal pressure. The further I got into my career, the more ideas I had, and eventually they piled-on to an already over-taxed brain. Writing was also a form of purging. The more I wrote, the better the jumbled thoughts in my racing brain were organized. My conversational impulses have tamed. I listen better.

I knew many of my ideas were quite different from those of my peers. I did not and still do not believe that they are all correct, but they are clearly different, and that makes me believe they might be useful.

Despite those personal side benefits, the main reason for *Wisdom Factories* is also the main reason for the career transformation I am in. I feel lucky. Though I spent my entire career (until 2022) in one place, I had the fortune of being in roles that fed my broad curiosities and exposed me to a wide variety of challenges and disciplines. For at least twenty of those years, I was responsible (among many others) for growing new business and science areas for the organization. That fed a deeply embedded curiosity drive, one that led me over and over toward breadth over depth. I got to understand a variety of fields, including aviation safety, biological and chemical defense, public health, health care, homeland security, disaster management, and several defense missions. I needed to keep up on the latest technical developments in areas from AI and software to bioscience and psychology. Related to this book, I had long viewed AI through the sometimes similar and often contrasting lenses of neuroscience and learning psychology. That perspective is unusual in both AI and education. I have borrowed enormously from many thinkers across many fields (only some of whom are referenced herein), but I think the residue of their ideas comes forth in this book in a unique combination.

Most importantly, I really do believe strongly that AI is creating many problems, that those problems will exacerbate, and that schools are stuck in the wrong place. Moving from AI research and development to the human side of the equation is a conscious choice based on where I think I'm most useful in the remainder of my career.

I want to thank some specific people for their contributions to this book and to my psyche as I've pursued it.

Annie Kip helped me find a path to my authentic work self through her unique and super-skilled coaching and strategy services (www.anniekip.com). I highly recommend seeking her help in your own transformation. She's responsible for the "wisdom" label; I was describing my ideas to her one day when she came back with "it sounds like you're talking about wisdom." I had been struggling with a unifying theme, and in that moment, she crystalized my thinking (reflecting her previous background in branding).

Dr. Mark DeFusco was initially an encouraging sounding board but has become a dear friend in the process. He has helped me through some tough times, and his ability to make others feel special is an incredible gift to me and the world.

Dr. Laura Gambino commented on sections of the book and publicity material, but her biggest contribution is helping me believe in myself as I transform. She has a brilliant mind and an even more radiant heart.

Several readers and collaborators helped make this a better book; any remaining errors and misrepresentations are solely my doing. Professor John Seater kept me...I hope...from making foolish economic pronouncements (it being a field I don't know much about). Dr. Robert Seater added important insights throughout. As the principal of a stellar set of game-oriented researchers that I worked with at MIT Lincoln Laboratory, and an inherently creative and deep-thinking soul, Rob was a key influence in how I think about games, analysis, and many other topics. Others in that camp include Adam Norige, Matthew Daggett, Jo Kurucar, and Dr. Hayley Davison Reynolds. Andrew Uhmeyer, Paul DiPastina, Nicole Lane, and Amanda Casale, among others, were important in design and development of many of the games. My AI influencers are many, but I owe special thanks to my dissertation advisor Dr. Evangelia "Litsa" Micheli-Tzanakou, and to Dr. Jason Thornton with whom I led an AI group for several years. Dr. Jim Evans had an outsized early-career influence on me in his emphasis on the human side of technology and leadership. "AKA iti" on Facebook generously volunteered to be a beta reader, and I'm thankful for her commentary. Dave Granchelli, Dr. Jason Thornton, Dr. Allison Chang, and Adam Norige helped me avoid sensitivities in mentions of my MIT Lincoln Laboratory career.

I thank the team of professionals who helped me get this book published, including K. J. Wetherholt (editing), "Bigpoints" on 99designs.com (cover), several people at Smith Publicity, Gwyn at GKS Creative (cover modification and file verification), and Bethany Brown at The Cadence Group (publishing). They led me through an unfamiliar process and gave warm and sage help. I recommend them highly.

Finally, I thank my family. Karen, Julia, and Rachel Dasey probably didn't always understand why I was writing so much in my supposed free time after work, but I knew I had their implicit support. I grew up with a bunch of really smart people: three sisters (Dr. Maureen Dasey-Morales, Mary Pardo, and Patricia Meyer) who put up with an annoying, overly competitive, and sometimes mischievous brother; and my parents John Dasey and Mary Dasey who fed my curiosities, never biased my chosen path, paid for much of my schooling even when it was financially difficult, and believed in me.

RECOMMENDED READING

J. E. Aoun, *Robot-Proof: Higher Education in the Age of Artificial Intelligence*, United Kingdom: MIT Press, 2018.

D. Buonomano, *Your Brain Is a Time Machine: The Neuroscience and Physics of Time*, United Kingdom: WW Norton, 2017.

B. Carey, *How We Learn: The Surprising Truth About When, Where, and Why It Happens,* United States: Random House Publishing Group, 2014.

S. Dehaene, *How We Learn: Why Brains Learn Better Than Any Machine...for Now,* United Kingdom: Penguin Publishing Group, 2021.

D. Epstein, *Range: Why Generalists Triumph in a Specialized World*, Italy: Penguin Publishing Group, 2021.

C. Goldin, C. D. Goldin, and L. K. Katz, *The Race Between Education and Technology,* United Kingdom: Harvard University Press, 2010.

A. Gopnik, *The Gardener and the Carpenter: What the New Science of Child Development Tells Us about the Relationship Between Parents and Children,* United Kingdom: "The" Bodley Head, 2016.

Y. N. Harari, *Homo Deus: A Brief History of Tomorrow*, Spain: HarperCollins, 2017.

D. Kahneman, *Thinking, Fast and Slow*, United States: Farrar, Straus and Giroux, 2011.

G. A. Klein, *Sources of Power: How People Make Decisions*, United States: MIT Press, 1999.

J. Kirby, and T. H. Davenport, *Only Humans Need Apply: Winners and Losers in the Age of Smart Machines*, United States: Harper-Collins, 2016.

A. McAfee, and E. Brynjolfsson, *The Second Machine Age: Work, Progress, and Prosperity in a Time of Brilliant Technologies*, United States: W. W. Norton, 2014.

I. McGilchrist, *The Master and His Emissary: The Divided Brain and the Making of the Western World*, New Haven: Yale University Press, 2009.

D. H. Meadows, *Thinking in Systems: A Primer*, United Kingdom: Chelsea Green Pub., 2008.

National Research Council, *How People Learn: Brain, Mind, Experience, and School: Expanded Edition*, Washington, DC: The National Academies Press, 2000.

J. J. Ratey, and E. M. Hallowell, *Driven to Distraction (Revised): Recognizing and Coping with Attention Deficit Disorder*, United Kingdom: Knopf Doubleday Publishing Group, 2011.

A. Ripley, *The Smartest Kids in the World: And How They Got That Way*, United Kingdom: Simon & Schuster, 2013.

K. Robinson, *Out of Our Minds: The Power of Being Creative*, Germany: Wiley, 2017.

P. E. Tetlock, and D. Gardner, *Superforecasting: The Art and Science of Prediction*, United States: Crown, 2015.

T. Wagner, and T. Dintersmith, *Most Likely to Succeed: Preparing Our Kids for the Innovation Era*, United Kingdom: Scribner, 2015.

NOTES AND REFERENCES

PROLOGUE

1 I. Asimov, *Isaac Asimov's Book of Science and Nature Quotations*, Edited by I. Asimov and J. A. Shulman, "Chapter 72: Science and Society," A Blue Cliff Editions Book: Weidenfeld & Nicolson, New York, pp. 281, 1988.

2 A. Mack, and I. Rock, *Inattentional Blindness*, Cambridge: Bradford, 1998.

3 D. J. Simons, and C. F. Chabris, "Gorillas in our midst: sustained inattentional blindness for dynamic events," *Perception*, Vol. 28, No. 9, pp. 1059–1074, 1999.

CHAPTER 1 – AI'S EXPERTISE TAKEOVER

4 A. McAfee, and E. Brynjolfsson, *The Second Machine Age: Work, Progress, and Prosperity in a Time of Brilliant Technologies*, United States: W. W. Norton, 2014.

5 N. Fox, *Against the Machines: The Hidden Luddite Tradition in Literature, Art and Individual Lives*, United States: Island Press, 2004.

6 T. Pynchon, "Is it O.K. to Be a Luddite?," In: *The New Romanticism: A Collection of Critical Essays, 1st edition*, E. Alsen, Ed., Abingdon: Routledge, 2000.

7 E. Andrews, "Who Were the Luddites?," *History*, Original: August 7, 2015, Updated: June 26, 2019. [Online] https://www.history.com/news/who-were-the-luddites. [Accessed Jan. 21, 2023].

8 K. Hill, "The Violent Opt-out: The Neo-Luddites Attacking Drones And Google Glass," *Forbes Tech*, [Online]

https://www.forbes.com/sites/kashmirhill/2014/07/15/the-violent-opt-out-people-destroying-drones-and-google-glass/#255efb283b61, July 15, 2014. [Accessed Jan. 21, 2023].

[9] L. Wronski and J. Cohen, "Workers worry about robots stealing jobs, just not their jobs. They may be overconfident," *Opinion – CNBC Work*, [Online] https://www.cnbc.com/2019/04/09/workers-worry-about-robots-stealing-jobs-just-not-their-jobs.html, April 9, 2019. [Accessed Jan. 21, 2023].

[10] I refer to technology as the chief change agent, but there are other factors that create work disruption. Globalization is another one. However, globalization is enabled in large part by technology, and the march of future technology like AI is a focus of the book. For simplicity, technology is the change agent I am emphasizing.

[11] A. Turing, "Intelligent Machinery, A Heretical Theory," a lecture he delivered in Manchester, England in 1951. His mother Sara published a draft of the lecture in *Alan M. Turing: Centenary Edition* by Sara Turing, *Chapter 14: Computing Machinery, Section: Intelligent Machinery, A Heretical Theory*, 2nd edition, Cambridge, England: Cambridge University Press, pg. 132, 2012. It is often mistakenly said that Turing predicted machine superiority over people, but the quote attributed to that view is "Once the machine thinking method had started, it would not take long to outstrip our feeble powers. At some stage therefore we should have to expect the machines to take control." He predicted that once machines could think that it would overtake people, but whether machines think remains debatable.

[12] M. Z. Bell, "Why Expert Systems Fail," *Journal of the Operational Research Society*, Vol. 36, No. 7, pp. 613-619, 1985.

[13] T. J. Dasey, and E. Micheli-Tzanakou, "An Unsupervised Neural Network System for Visual Evoked Potentials," a chapter in *Supervised and Unsupervised Pattern Recognition*, 1st *edition*, E. Micheli-Tzanakou, *et al.,* Eds., Boca Raton: CRC Press, pp. 185-194, 2000.

[14] A. Krizhevsky, I. Sutskever, and G. E. Hinton, "ImageNet Classification with Deep Convolutional Neural Networks," *Proceedings of the 25th International Conference on Neural Information Processing Systems*, Lake Tahoe, NV, pp. 1097–1105, 2012.

[15] A. Vaswani, N. Shazeer, N. Palmer, J. Uszkoreit, L. Jones, A. N. Gomez, L. Kaiser, and I. Polosukhin, "Attention is All you need," *ArXiv*, https://arxiv.org/abs/1706.03762, 2017.

[16] A. Rao, "Why the new AI/ML language model GPT-3 is a big deal," [Online] https://raohacker.com/why-the-new-ai-nlp-language-model-gpt-3-is-a-big-deal/, August, 2000. [Accessed Feb. 16, 2023.]

[17] T. Brown, *et al.,* "Language Models are Few-Shot Learners," *arXiv*, https://arxiv.org/pdf/2005.14165.pdf, Jul. 22, 2020

[18] K. Roose, "How ChatGPT Kicked Off an A.I. Arms Race," *New York Times,* [Online] https://www.nytimes.com/2023/02/03/technology/chatgpt-openai-artificial-intelligence.html, Feb. 3, 2023. [Accessed Feb. 16, 2023.]

[19] B. Marr, "The Best Examples of What You can Do With ChatGPT," *Forbes*, [Online] https://www.forbes.com/sites/bernard-marr/2023/03/01/the-best-examples-of-what-you-can-do-with-chatgpt, March 1, 2023. [Accessed March 7, 2023.]

[20] OpenAI, "DALL•E 2," *OpenAI*, Online] https://openai.com/dall-e-2/, 2023. [Accessed Jan. 21, 2023.]

[21] Thema Newsroom, "Instagram hits 1 billion monthly users! (infographic)," *themanews.com*, [Online] https://en.protothema.gr/instagram-hits-1-billion-monthly-users-infographic/, June 21, 2018. [Accessed Feb. 16, 2023.]

[22] D. Højris Bæk, "ChatGPT User Statistics & Facts (100 million users reached in January 2023)," *SEO.ai*, [Online] https://seo.ai/blog/chatgpt-user-statistics-facts, Feb. 3, 2023. [Accessed Feb. 16, 2023.]

[23] A. Gairola, "Noam Chomsky Slams ChatGPT: 'High Tech Plagiarism' With No Benefits for Education," *MSN*, [Online] https://www.msn.com/en-us/money/news/noam-chomsky-slams-chatgpt-high-tech-plagiarism-with-no-benefits-for-education/ar-AA17pszK, Feb. 13, 2023. [Accessed Feb. 16, 2023.]

[24] *Hard Fork* podcast, "Bing's Revenge and Google's A.I. Face-Plant," *New York Times*, [Online] https://www.nytimes.com/2023/02/10/podcasts/bings-revenge-and-googles-ai-face-plant.html?showTranscript=1, Feb. 10, 2023. [Accessed Feb. 16, 2023.]

[25] R. Morrison, "GPT-4 will 'leave people disappointed' says OpenAI CEO," *Tech Monitor*, [Online] https://techmonitor.ai/technology/ai-and-automation/gpt-4-openai-chatgpt-sam-altman, Jan. 19, 2023. [Accessed Feb. 16, 2023.]

[26] S. Sundar, and A. Mok, "Sam Altman unveils the hotly anticipated GPT-4, an AI model he says 'can pass a bar exam and score a 5 on several AP exams'," *Insider,* [Online] https://www.businessinsider.com/gpt-4-openai-model-api-details-2023-3, March 14, 2023. [Accessed April 23, 2023.]

[27] J. Vincent, "Tencent says there are only 300,000 AI engineers worldwide, but millions are needed," *The Verge,* [Online] https://www.theverge.com/2017/12/5/16737224/global-ai-talent-shortfall-tencent-report, December 5, 2017. [Accessed March 20, 2023.]

[28] B. Zoph, V. Vasudevan, J. Schlens, and Q. V. Le, "Learning Transferable Architectures for Scalable Image Recognition," *ArXiv,* https://arxiv.org/pdf/1707.07012.pdf, April 11, 2018. Note that my memory is weak regarding which research was presented in the seminar. This paper may be the right project, but if not it is representative of state-of-the-art at the time.

[29] Y. Li, *et al.,* "Competition-level code generation with AlphaCode," *Science,* Vol. 378, No. 6624, pp. 1092-1097, 2022.

[30] G. Doherty, M. Musolesi, A. Sano and T. Vaessen, "Mental State, Mood, and Emotion," *IEEE Pervasive Computing,* Vol. 21, No. 02, pp. 8-9, 2022. This special issue contains several articles which are representative of current state-of-the-art in wearable physiological monitoring.

[31] R. Gonzalez, "Virtual Therapists Help Veterans Open Up About PTSD: An artificially intelligent therapist named Ellie helps members of the military open up about their mental health," *WIRED,* [Online] https://www.wired.com/story/virtual-therapists-help-veterans-open-up-about-ptsd, Oct. 17, 2017. [Accessed Jan. 21, 2023].

[32] L. Nedelkoska, and G. Quintini, "Automation, skills use and training," *OECD Social, Employment and Migration Working Papers,* No. 202, Paris: OECD Publishing, [Online] https://doi.org/10.1787/2e2f4eea-en, 2018. [Accessed Jan. 21, 2023].

[33] A. K. Bartscher, M. Kuhn, and M. Schularick, "The College Wealth Divide Continues to Grow," *Economic Synopses,* No. 1, 2020.

[34] C. Goldin, L. F. Katz, and C. D. Goldin, *The Race Between Education and Technology,* Cambridge: Harvard University Press, 2008.

CHAPTER 2 – HUMANITY'S WISDOM ROLE

[35] B. F. Skinner, *Contingencies of Reinforcement: A Theoretical Analysis*, B. F. Skinner Foundation, 2014.

[36] J. Lehrer, "Do Political Experts Know What They're Talking About?," *WIRED*, [Online] https://www.wired.com/2011/08/do-political-experts-know-what-theyre-talking-about/, Aug. 4, 2011. [Accessed Jan. 21, 2023.]

[37] Prediction and forecasting are not synonymous terms. Forecasting is more precise and scorable. Professor Tetlock says he does work on forecasting rather than prediction. I am using the terms interchangeably according to colloquial use.

[38] P. E. Tetlock, *Expert Political Judgment: How Good Is It? How Can We Know?—New Edition*, United Kingdom: Princeton University Press, 2017.

[39] D. Gardner, and P. E. Tetlock, *Superforecasting: The Art and Science of Prediction*, United States: Crown, 2015.

[40] I. Berlin, *The hedgehog and the fox : an essay on Tolstoy's view of history*, Chicago: Ivan R. Dee, Publisher, 1993. Originally published in 1953.

[41] P. Tetlock, "Why Foxes Are Better Forecasters Than Hedgehogs," Seminar for the *Long Now Foundation*, [Online] https://www.youtube.com/watch?v=EeHyVauX458, Jan. 26, 2007. [Accessed Jan. 21, 2023.]

[42] R. Conniff, "What the Luddites Really Fought Against," *Smithsonian Magazine*, [Online] https://www.smithsonianmag.com/history/what-the-luddites-really-fought-against-264412/, March, 2011. [Accessed Jan. 21, 2023.]

[43] E. Klein, and S. Locke, "40 maps that explain food in America," *Vox*, [Online] https://www.vox.com/a/explain-food-america, June 9, 2014. [Accessed Jan. 21, 2023.]

[44] The National Commission on Excellence in Education, "A Nation at Risk : the Imperative for Educational Reform," *United States Department of Education*, Washington, D.C.: National Commission on Excellence in Education, [Superintendent of Documents, U.S. Government Printing Office distributor], 1983.

[45] A. Kamenetz, "What 'A Nation At Risk' Got Wrong, And Right, About U.S. Schools," *NPR*, [Online] https://www.npr.org/sections/ed/2018/04/29/604986823/what-a-nation-at-risk-got-wrong-and-right-about-u-s-schools, April 28, 2018. [Accessed Jan. 21, 2023.]

[46] L. Stedman, "The Sandia Report and U.S. Achievement: An Assessment," *The Journal of Educational Research*, Vol. 87, pp. 133-146, 1994.

[47] *No Child Left Behind Act of 2001*, P.L. 107-110, 20 U.S.C. § 6319, 2002.

[48] *Every Student Succeeds Act*, 20 U.S.C. § 6301, 2015.

[49] The Secretary's Commission on Achieving Necessary Skills, "What work requires of schools: A SCANS report for America 2000," Washington DC: U.S. Department of Labor, 1991.

[50] BattelleforKids, "Frameworks & Resources," [Online] https://www.battelleforkids.org/networks/p21/frameworks-resources, accessed Jan. 21, 2023.

[51] "Common Core State Standards," *Council of Chief State School Officers*, [Online] https://learning.ccsso.org/common-core-state-standards-initiative, accessed Jan. 21, 2023.

[52] A. Taylor, J. Nelson, S. O'Donnell, E. Davies, and J. Hillary, *The Skills Imperative 2035: what does the literature tell us about essential skills most needed for work?-Working Paper 1*, Slough: NFER (National Foundation for Educational Research), [Online] https://files.eric.ed.gov/fulltext/ED619280.pdf, 2022. [Accessed Jan. 21, 2023].

[53] D. Buonomano, *Your Brain Is a Time Machine: The Neuroscience and Physics of Time*, United Kingdom: W. W. Norton, 2017.

[54] J. D. Webster, "Self-report wisdom measures: Strengths, limitations, and future directions," In: *The Cambridge Handbook of Wisdom*, R. J. Sternberg & J. Glück (Eds.), Cambridge: Cambridge University Press, pp. 297-320, 2019.

[55] Meta Fundamental AI Research (FAIR) Diplomacy Team, *et al.*, "Human-level play in the game of Diplomacy by combining language models with strategic reasoning," *Science*, Vol. 378, No. 6624, pp. 1067-1074, 2022.

CHAPTER 3 – WICKED COMPLEXITY

[56] L. J. Peter, *Peter's Almanac*, United States: Morrow, 1982.

[57] R. Poli, "A Note on the Difference Between Complicated and Complex Social Systems," *CADMUS Journal*, Vol. 2, No. 1, pp. 142-147, October, 2013.

[58] D. H. Meadows, *Thinking in Systems: A Primer*, United Kingdom: Chelsea Green Publishing, 2008.

[59] R. Nason, *It's Not Complicated: The Art and Science of Complexity in Business*, United Kingdom: University of Toronto Press, 2017.

[60] A. R. Jensen, "How Much Can We Boost IQ and Scholastic Achievement," *Harvard Educational Review*, Vol. 39, pp. 1-123, 1969.

[61] There is work by other researchers that show the rate of change of IQ scores is decreasing in the past few decades, and even reversing a bit in some parts of the industrialized world. However, the general principle of long-term IQ score increases is not widely disputed.

[62] C. Shea, "IQ Wars Continue With Battles Over New Puzzles," *The Chronicle of Higher Education*, [Online] https://www.chronicle.com/article/iq-wars-continue-with-battles-over-new-puzzles/, October 29, 2012. [Accessed Feb. 23, 2023.]

[63] R. E. Nisbett, C. Blair, W. Dickens, J. Flynn, D. F. Halpern, and E. Turkheimer, "Intelligence: New findings and theoretical developments," *American Psychologist*, Vol. 67, No. 2, pp. 130-159, 2012.

[64] J. Weissmann, "Here's How Little Math Americans Actually Use at Work," *The Atlantic*, [Online] https://www.theatlantic.com/business/archive/2013/04/heres-how-little-math-americans-actually-use-at-work/275260/, April 24, 2013. [Accessed March 5, 2023.]

[65] V. Amrhein, S. Greenland, and B. McShane, "Scientists rise up against statistical significance," *Nature*, [Online] https://www.nature.com/articles/d41586-019-00857-9, March 20, 2019. [Accessed Jan. 25, 2023.]

[66] B. A. Simonsmeier, M. Flaig, A. Deiglmayr, L. Schalk, and M. Schneider, "Domain-specific prior knowledge and learning: A meta-analysis," *Educational Psychologist*, Vol. 57, No. 1, pp. 31-54, 2022.

[67] G. Brod, "Toward an understanding of when prior knowledge helps or hinders learning," *npj Sci. Learn*, Vol. 6, No. 24, 2021.

[68] R. Bohn, and J. Short, "Measuring Consumer Information," *Intl. Journal of Communication*, Vol. 6, pp. 980-1000, 2012.

⁶⁹ A. Ali, "How Media Consumption Has Changed Over the Last Decade," *Visual Capitalist*, [Online] https://www.visualcapitalist.com/how-media-consumption-has-changed-in-2021/, April 28, 2021. [Accessed March 3, 2023.]

⁷⁰ M. Wolf, "Skim reading is the new normal. The effect on society is profound," *The Guardian*, [Online] https://www.theguardian.com/commentisfree/2018/aug/25/skim-reading-new-normal-maryanne-wolf, August 25, 2018. [Accessed March 4, 2023.]

⁷¹ H. Rittel, and M. Webber, "Dilemmas in a General Theory of Planning," *Policy Sciences*, Vol. 4, No. 2, pp. 155-169, 1973.

⁷² J. Conklin, *Dialogue mapping: building shared understanding of wicked problems*, Chichester, England: Wiley, 2006.

CHAPTER 4 – THE ROOTS OF WISDOM

⁷³ Einstein spoke of intuition often, but this is likely a paraphrase of his views and not a direct quote. The website *Quote Investigator* (https://quoteinvestigator.com/2013/09/18/intuitive-mind/) suggests the 1976 book *The Metaphoric Mind: A Celebration of Creative Consciousness* by Bob Samples (p. 26) may be the initial source. Samples was not expressing a quote but rather summarizing Einstein's views.

⁷⁴ D. Ryan, "Taking games seriously at the Lincoln Laboratory," *MIT News*, [Online] https://news.mit.edu/2013/taking-games-seriously, September 23, 2013. [Accessed April 24, 2023.]

⁷⁵ T. Dasey, "Public Safety in the Information Age," Presentation at the *Harvard Public Safety Summit*, April 26, 2015. Information about the Summit can also be found at "Leadership for a New Era: Insights from the 2015 Public Safety Summit at Harvard University," Leadership for a Networked World, *Harvard University Kennedy School*, [Online] https://lnwprogram.org/sites/default/files/Public_Safety_Report_2015.pdf, 2015. [Accessed Jan. 22, 2023].

⁷⁶ M. B. Miller, W. Sinnott-Armstrong, L. Young, D. King, A. Paggi, M. Fabri, G. Polonara, and M. S. Gazzaniga, "Abnormal moral reasoning in complete and partial callosotomy patients," *Neuropsychologia*, Vol. 48, pp. 2215–2220, 2010.

[77] R. W. Sperry, M. S. Gazzaniga, and J. E. Bogen, "Interhemispheric relationships: the neocortical commissures; syndromes of hemisphere disconnection," *Handb Clin Neurol*, Vol. 4, pp. 273-290, 1969.

[78] D. Wolman, "A Tale of Two Halves," *Nature*, Vol. 483, pp. 260-263, 2012.

[79] J. D. Schmahmann, "The cerebellum and cognition," *Neuroscience Letters*, Vol. 688, pp. 62-75, 2019.

[80] R. Swain, A. Kerr, and R. Thompson, "The Cerebellum: A Neural System for the Study of Reinforcement Learning," *Frontiers in behavioral neuroscience*, Vol. 5, No. 8, 2011.

[81] A. W. Young, Ed., *Functions of the Right Cerebral Hemisphere*, London: Academic Press, 1983.

[82] T. Vilasboas, H. Guillaume Herbet, and D. Hugues, "Challenging the Myth of Right Nondominant Hemisphere: Lessons from Corticosubcortical Stimulation Mapping in Awake Surgery and Surgical Implications," *World Neurosurgery*, Vol. 103, pp. 449-456, 2017.

[83] O. Güntürkün, F. Ströckens, and S. Ocklenburg, "Brain Lateralization: A Comparative Perspective," *Physiol Rev.*, Vol. 100, No. 3, pp. 1019-1063, 2020.

[84] E. Frasnelli, "Brain and behavioral lateralization in invertebrates," *Front Psychol*, Vol 4, pp. 939, 2013.

[85] A. Toga, and P. Thompson, "Mapping brain asymmetry," *Nat Rev Neurosci*, Vol. 4, pp. 37–48, 2003.

[86] R. Carter, *Mapping the mind*, Berkeley, CA: University of California Press, 1999.

[87] R. G. Carson, "Inter-hemispheric inhibition sculpts the output of neural circuits by co-opting the two cerebral hemispheres," *The Journal of Physiology*, Vol. 598, No. 21, pp. 4781-4802, 2020.

[88] K. Perina, "Kim Peek, the Real Rain Man: Low IQ, extraordinary mind," *Psychology Today*, [Online] https://www.psychologytoday.com/ca/blog/the-superhuman-mind/201212/kim-peek-the-real-rain-man, Dec. 11, 2012. [Accessed Jan. 23, 2023].

[89] I. McGilchrist, *The Master and His Emissary: The Divided Brain and the Making of the Western World*, New Haven: Yale University Press, 2009.

[90] L. J. Rogers, and G. Kaplan, "An Eye for a Predator: Lateralization in Birds, with Particular Reference to the Australian Magpie," In: *Behavioural and Morphological Asymmetries in Vertebrates*, Y. Malashichev, and A. W. Deckel, Eds., Landes Bioscience, pp. 47-57, 2006.

[91] N. Marinsek, B. O. Turner, M. Gazzaniga, and M. B. Miller, "Divergent hemispheric reasoning strategies: reducing uncertainty versus resolving inconsistency," *Frontiers in Human Neuroscience*, Vol. 8, 2014.

[92] M. Johnson, "Psychology of the Left Hemisphere: The Brain's Interpreter," *Psychology Today*, [Online] https://www.psychologytoday.com/us/blog/mind-brain-and-value/202008/psychology-the-left-hemisphere-the-brains-interpreter, August 11, 2020. [Accessed Jan. 23, 2023.]

[93] A. Matsuura, "Personality assessments in the workplace: harmful or helpful?," *The Daily Universe, Brigham Young University*, [Online] https://universe.byu.edu/2019/12/11/personality-assessments-in-the-workplace-harmful-or-helpful/, Dec. 11, 2019. [Accessed Jan. 23, 2023.]

[94] A. Schofield, "The brains of leadership and management," *LeadershipReview*, [Online] https://www.leadershipreview.net/the-brains-of-leadership-and-management/, accessed April 27, 2023.

[95] P. Rosenzweig, *The Halo Effect: ...and the Eight Other Business Delusions That Deceive Managers*, United Kingdom: Free Press, 2014.

[96] D. L. Paulhus, and K. Williams, "The Dark Triad of personality: Narcissism, Machiavellianism and psychopathy," *Journal of Research in Personality*, Vol. 36, No. 6, pp. 556–563, 2002.

[97] A. Furnham, and S. C. Richards, "The Dark Triad of Personality: A 10 Year Review," *Social and Personality Psychology Compass*, Vol. 7, No. 3, pp. 199–216, 2013.

[98] W. K. Campbell, and J. M. Twenge, "Narcissism Unleashed," *Association for Psychological Science*, [Online] https://www.psychologicalscience.org/observer/narcissism-unleashed, November 27, 2013. [Accessed Jan. 23, 2023.]

[99] S. J. Diller, A. Czibor, Z. P. Szabó, *et al.*, "The positive connection between dark triad traits and leadership levels in self- and other-ratings," *Leadersh Educ Personal Interdiscip J*, Vol. 3, pp. 117–131, 2021.

[100] M. Z. Bell, "Why Expert Systems Fail," *Journal of the Operational Research Society*, Vol. 36, No. 7, pp. 613-619, 1985.

101 J. A. Russell, "Core affect and the psychological construction of emotion," *Psychological review*, Vol. 110, No. 1, pp. 145–172, 2003.

102 Scale-free network, *Wikipedia*, https://en.wikipedia.org/wiki/Scale-free_network, accessed Jan. 23, 2023.

103 C. S. Soon, M. Brass, H. J. Heinze, and J. D. Haynes, "Unconscious determinants of free decisions in the human brain." *Nature neuroscience*, Vol. 11, No. 5, pp. 543–545, 2008.

CHAPTER 5 – EXPERIENCE

104 R. M. Brown, *Alma Mate*r, United Kingdom: Ballantine Books, 2002.

105 C. Homans, "War Games: A Short History," *FP,* [Online] https://foreignpolicy.com/2011/08/31/war-games-a-short-history/, Aug. 31, 2011. [Accessed April 25, 2023.]

106 C. von Clausewitz, *On War*, United Kingdom: Princeton University Press, 1989.

107 DHS Science and Technology Directorate, "Next-Generation Incident Command System," [Online] https://www.dhs.gov/sites/default/files/publications/Next%20Generation%20Incident%20Command%20System-NICS_0.pdf, 2014. [Accessed April 25, 2023.]

108 J. Verrico, "News Release: NICS, A Communication Platform for First Responders, Now Available Worldwide." *DHS S&T Press Office, U.S. Department of Homeland Security (DHS)*, [Online] https://www.dhs.gov/science-and-technology/news/2016/08/08/news-release-nics-communication-platform-first-responders-now, Aug. 8, 2016. [Accessed April 25, 2023.]

109 G. A. Klein, R. Calderwood, and A. Clinton-Cirocco, "Rapid Decision Making on the Fire Ground," *Proceedings of the Human Factors Society Annual Meeting*, Vol. 30, No. 6, pp. 576–580, 1986.

110 W. C. Howell, "Task Influences in the Analytic-Intuitive Approach to Decision Making," *Defense Technical Information Center (DTIC)*, Report DTIC_ADA149870, [Online] https://apps.dtic.mil/dtic/tr/fulltext/u2/a149870.pdf, 1984.

111 D. Kahneman, *Thinking, Fast and Slow*, United States: Farrar, Straus and Giroux, 2011.

112 G. A. Klein, *Sources of Power: How People Make Decisions,* United States: MIT Press, 1999.

[113] H. Gruber, "Qualitative Aspekte von Expertise im Schach [Qualitative aspects of expertise in chess]," Aachen: Feenschach, Doctoral dissertation, 1991.

[114] G. A. Klein, *Intuition at Work: Why Developing Your Gut Instincts Will Make You Better at what You Do*, United States: Currency/Doubleday, 2003.

[115] G. Klein, "A naturalistic decision making perspective on studying intuitive decision making," *Journal of Applied Research in Memory and Cognition*, Vol. 4, No. 3, pp. 164-168, 2015.

[116] The term of art is usually knowledge graphs rather than knowledge networks, but the term graph is confusing outside of math circles. Graph theory is math about associative networks. "Graph" doesn't refer to X-Y or any other kind of plot.

[117] B. Hart, and T. R. Riley, *Meaningful Differences in the Everyday Experience of Young American Children*, Baltimore, MD: Paul H. Brooks Publishing Co., 1995.

[118] B. Hart, and T. R. Risley, "The Early Catastrophe: The 30 Million Word Gap by Age 3," *American Educator*, American Federation of Teachers (AFT), [Online] https://www.aft.org/ae/spring2003/hart_risley, Spring 2003. [Accessed Jan. 24, 2023.]

[119] Wealth itself isn't likely the cause. Rather, the behavior of parents is thought to be causative, and that can have many factors. Among the differences noted in socioeconomically disadvantaged families are less parent time with children, less speaking when together, fewer words and concepts used, and more discouraging than encouraging feedback to kids.

[120] American Psychological Association, "Education and Socioeconomic Status," [Online] https://www.apa.org/pi/ses/resources/publications/education, July 2017. [Accessed Jan. 24, 2023.]

[121] E. Shafir, and S. Mullainathan, *Scarcity: Why Having Too Little Means So Much*, United States: Henry Holt and Company, 2013.

[122] P. McGrath, and F. Elgar, "Effects of Socio-Economic Status on Behavioral Problems," In: *International Encyclopedia of the Social and Behavioral Sciences, Volume 1*, J. D. Wright (Ed.), India: Elsevier Science, 2015.

[123] OpenAI, "GPT-4 Technical Report," *ArXiv*, https://arxiv.org/abs/2303.08774, March 15, 2023.

[124] WYSE News, "Travel improves educational attainment & future success," *WYSE Travel Confederation*, [Online] https://www.wysetc.org/2013/10/travel-improves-educational-attainment-future-success, Oct. 24, 2013. [Accessed Jan. 24, 2023.]

[125] P. Gosselin, "If You're Over 50, Chances are the Decision to Leave a Job Won't be Yours," *ProPublica*, [Online] https://www.propublica.org/article/older-workers-united-states-pushed-out-of-work-forced-retirement, December 28, 2018. [Accessed Jan. 24, 2023.]

[126] M. Barabasi, "What your age really says about your chance of success at work," *TED Radio Hour,* NPR, [Online] https://www.npr.org/2022/11/11/1137466873/what-your-age-really-says-about-your-chance-of-success-at-work, Nov. 18, 2022.

CHAPTER 6 – THE GAME CHANGER

[127] D. Ackerman, *Deep Play*, United States: Knopf Doubleday Publishing Group, 2000.

[128] PrepScholar, "MIT Requirements for Admission," [Online] https://www.prepscholar.com/sat/s/colleges/MIT-admission-requirements, accessed Jan. 25, 2023.

[129] M. Stains, J. Harshman, *et al.*, "Anatomy of STEM teaching in North American universities," *Science*, Vol. 359, No. 6383, pp. 1468, 2018.

[130] MIT iCampus, "TEAL – Technology Enabled Active Learning," [Online] https://icampus.mit.edu/projects/teal/, accessed Jan. 25, 2023.

[131] R. Beichner, "The Student-Centered Active Learning Environment for Undergraduate Programs (SCALE-UP) Project, [Online] https://www.researchgate.net/profile/Robert-Beichner/publication/253489519_The_Student-Centered_Active_Learning_Environment_for_Undergraduate_Programs_SCALE-UP_Project/links/00b7d53c56fbe50009000000/The-Student-Centered-Active-Learning-Environment-for-Undergraduate-Programs-SCALE-UP-Project.pdf, 2011.

[132] Y. J. Dori, and J. Belcher, "How Does Technology-Enabled Active Learning Affect Undergraduate Students' Understanding of Electromagnetism Concepts?," *The Journal of the Learning Sciences*, Vol. 14, No. 2, pp. 243-279, 2005.

133 T. Dasey, "The Design and Motivation for the Integrated Terminal Weather System Microburst Detection Algorithm," *American Institute of Aeronautics and Astronautics (AIAA) Aircraft Design, Systems and Operations Meeting*, Monterey, CA, publication AIAA-93-3948, Aug. 11-13, 1993.

134 National Center for Atmospheric Research (NCAR), "Low-Level Wind Shear Alert System (LLWAS)," [Online] https://ral.ucar.edu/solutions/products/low-level-wind-shear-alert-system-llwas, accessed April 25, 2023.

135 R. Seater, "Rapid-Play Serious Games for Technology Triage," *Lincoln Laboratory Journal*, Vol. 23, No. 1, pp. 71-80, [Online] https://www.ll.mit.edu/sites/default/files/publication/doc/2019-05/23_7_Seater_Rapid-Play%20Serious%20Games_2019_122434.pdf, 2019.

136 D. Whitebread, D. Neale, H. Jensen, C. Liu, L. Solis, E. Hopkins, K. Hirsh-Pasek, and J. Zosh, "The role of play in children's development: a review of the evidence," *The LEGO Foundation*, Nov. 2017.

137 This quote is widely attributed to Mr. Rogers, but I could not find the exact source of the comment.

138 D. A. Redelmeier, and D. Kahneman, "Patients' memories of painful medical treatments: real-time and retrospective evaluations of two minimally invasive procedures," *Pain*, Vol. 66, No. 1, pp. 3–8, 1996.

139 D. A. Redelmeier, J. Katz, and D. Kahneman, "Memories of colonoscopy: a randomized trial," *Pain*, Vol. 104, No. 1, pp. 187-194, 2003.

140 A. Bacon, C. Walsh, and L. Martin, "Fantasy proneness and counterfactual thinking," *Personality and Individual Differences*, Vol. 54, pp. 469–473, 2013.

141 L. Alfieri, T. J. Nokes-Malach, and C. D. Schunn, "Learning Through Case Comparisons: A Meta-Analytic Review," *Educational Psychologist*, Vol. 48, No. 2, pp. 87-113, 2013.

142 M. L. Gick, and K. J. Holyoak, "Schema induction and analogical transfer," *Cognitive Psychology*, Vol. 15, No. 1, pp. 1–38, 1983.

143 R. J. Beck, and J. Harter, "Why Great Managers Are So Rare," *Harvard Business Review*, [Online] https://hbr.org/2014/03/why-good-managers-are-so-rare, March 13, 2014. [Accessed Jan. 25, 2023.]

144 J. Zenger, and J. Folkman, "Why the Most Productive People Don't Always Make the Best Managers," *Harvard Business Review*, [Online] https://hbr.org/2018/04/why-the-most-productive-people-dont-always-make-the-best-managers, April 17, 2018. [Accessed Jan. 25, 2023.]

145 R. Seater, "Rapid Play Digitial Games for Emergency Management Instruction," In: *Simulation and Game-Based Learning in Emergency and Disaster Management*, United States: IGI Global, pp. 63-95, 2021.

146 Unity, "How to Make a Video game Without Any Coding Experience," [Online] https://unity.com/how-to/make-games-without-programming, accessed Jan. 25, 2023.

147 V. Goncharenko, "ChatGPT learns massively multiplayer online game development," *Metaverse Post*, [Online] https://mpost.io/chatgpt-learns-massively-multiplayer-online-game-development/, Dec. 15, 2022. [Accessed Jan. 25, 2023.]

148 P. J. Denning, and M. Tedre, *Computational Thinking*, Cambridge, MA: The MIT Press, 2019.

149 The evaluation evidence would derive from student performance differences between the beginning and the end of the course. This is a practical choice that completely ignores longer-term conceptual gains. Our associative network keeps going. Leaps of insight are often delayed or become cemented only when revisited after a time gap.

150 B. Flicklinger, *Reward Learning with Badges: Spark Student Achievement*, United Kingdom: International Society for Technology in Education, 2016.

151 I. Granic, A. Lobel, and R. C. M. E. Engels, "The Benefits of Playing Video Games," *American Psychologist*, Vol. 69, No. 1, pp. 66-78, Jan. 2014.

152 A. Hallur, "21+ Truly Shocking Online Course Completion Rate Statistics," *BloggingX*, [Online] https://bloggingx.com/online-course-completion-statistics/, Oct. 5, 2022. [Accessed Jan. 25, 2023.]

153 A. Guttmann, "Estimated media revenue worldwide in 2020, by category," *Statistica*, [Online] https://www.statista.com/statistics/1132706/media-revenue-worldwide/ Jan. 17, 2022. [Accessed Jan. 25, 2023.]

CHAPTER 7 – UPSIDE-DOWN SCHOOLING

[154] J. Dewey, *Democracy and Education: An Introduction to the Philosophy of Education*, United States: Macmillan, pp. 168, 1916.

[155] "Horace Mann: American Educator," *Encyclopedia Britannica,* https://www.britannica.com/biography/Horace-Mann, accessed Jan. 26, 2023. This reference was used for all of the biographical facts mentioned in this writing. Interpretations of his work and influence stem from other publications, or from the author, as indicated.

[156] Wikipedia, "Horace Mann," https://en.wikipedia.org/wiki/Horace_Mann, accessed Jan. 25, 2023. These words or similar ones appear in several publications, though I cannot find an original source. Nevertheless, they are consistent with Mann's philosophies as documented in many works.

[157] Under Mann's tenure, the first women's colleges—called normal schools—were formed to develop new teachers. He believed women were better teachers. Mann was a vociferous abolitionist. African Americans were also educated, though not with the same vigor, in the same schools, or with the same material (e.g., grammar instruction was forbidden). In 1857 the Massachusetts legislature passed a law desegregating public schools. Some would argue that remains unimplemented.

[158] "Horace Mann: American Educator," *Encyclopedia.com,* https://www.encyclopedia.com/social-sciences/news-wires-white-papers-and-books/education-reform-movement, accessed Jan. 26, 2023.

[159] T. A. Guzman, "The Power to Oversee the Education System, A Historical Timeline from the Prussian Empire to the Rockefeller Dynasty," *Astute News: The Science of News and Analysis*, [Online] https://astutenews.com/2019/09/the-power-to-oversee-the-education-system-a-historical-timeline-from-the-prussian-empire-to-the-rockefeller-dynasty, Sept. 3, 2019. [Accessed Jan. 25, 2023.]

[160] V. J. Anderson, *The Other Eminent Men of Wilford Woodruff*, Nelson Book, 2000. Found online at Joseph Smith Foundation, "Frederick the Great," https://josephsmithfoundation.org/frederick-the-great/, which shows the relevant section in Ms. Anderson's book.

[161] History.com editors, "Frederick II," *HISTORY*, A&E Television Net [Online] https://www.history.com/topics/germany/frederick-ii-prussia, last updated Jan. 11, 2023. [Accessed Jan. 25, 2023.]

[162] J. T. Gatto, *The Underground History of American Education*, Sydney, Australia: Odysseus Group, 2000.

[163] V. Trowler, "Student engagement literature review," *The higher education academy*, Vol. 11, No. 1, pp. 1-15, 2010.

[164] Gallup, "Engagement Today – Ready for Tomorrow: Fall 2015 survey results," Washington, DC, 2016.

[165] C. Pulfrey, C. Buchs, and F. Butera, "Why grades engender performance-avoidance goals: The mediating role of autonomous motivation," *Journal of Educational Psychology*, Vol. 103, No. 3, pp. 683-700, 2011.

[166] M. H. Nichols, and K. Cator, "Challenge Based Learning White Paper," Cupertino, California: Apple, Inc., [Online] https://www.challenge-basedlearning.org/wp-content/uploads/2019/03/CBL_Paper_2008.pdf, 2008. [Accessed Jan. 25, 2023.]

[167] L. Johnson, and S. Adams, "Challenge Based Learning: The Report from the Implementation Project," *New Media Consortium*, [Online] https://files.eric.ed.gov/fulltext/ED532404.pdf, 2011. [Accessed Jan. 25, 2023.]

[168] S. Kohn, Ed., *Ungrading: Why Rating Students Undermines Learning (and What to Do Instead)*, United States: West Virginia University Press, 2020.

[169] Code.org, CSTA, & ECEP Alliance, "2022 State of Computer Science Education: Understanding Our National Imperative," retrieved from https://advocacy.code.org/stateofcs, 2022.

CHAPTER 8 – PRODUCTIVITY THERAPY

[170] D. R. Mortensen, "Artificial Intelligence is About to Make Us All Managers. But Are We Ready?," *Trello*, [Online] https://blog.trello.com/artificial-intelligence-is-about-to-make-us-all-managers, August 10, 2017. [Accessed Jan. 26, 2023.]

[171] B. Jones, "The mystery of the mimic plant," *Vox*, [Online] https://www.vox.com/down-to-earth/2022/11/30/23473062/plant-mimicry-boquila-trifoliolata, Jan. 11, 2023. [Accessed Jan. 26, 2023.]

[172] E. Gianoli, and F. Carrasco-Urra, "Leaf Mimicry in a Climbing Plan Protects Against Herbivory," *Current Biology*, Vol. 24, pp. 984-987, 2014.

[173] E. D. Brenner, R. Stahlberg, S. Mancuso, J. Vivanco, F. Baluška, and E. Van Volkenburgh, "Plant neurobiology: an integrated view of plant signaling," *Trends in Plant Science*, Vol. 11, No. 8, pp. 413-419, 2006.

[174] A. Alpi, N. Amrhein, *et al.*, "Plant neurobiology: no brain, no gain?," *Trends in Plant Science*, Vol. 12, No. 4, pp. 135–6, April 2007.

[175] L. Taiz, D. Alkon, A. Draguhn, A. Murphy, M. Blatt, C. Hawes, G. Thiel, and D. G. Robinson, "Plants Neither Possess nor Require Consciousness," *Trends in Plant Science*, Vol. 24, No. 8, pp. 677-687, 2019.

[176] J. White, and F. Yamashita, "*Boquila trifoliolata* mimics leaves of an artificial plastic host plant," *Plant Signaling & Behavior*, Vol. 17, No. 1, 2022.

[177] A. Trewavas, "Response to Alpi *et al.*: Plant neurobiology—all metaphors have value," *Trends in Plant Science*, Vol. 12, No. 6, pp. 231–3, 2007.

[178] E. Gent, "Artificial Intelligence is evolving all by itself: Advance replicates decades of AI research in days," *Science*, [Online] https://www.science.org/content/article/artificial-intelligence-evolving-all-itself, April 13, 2020. [Accessed Jan. 26, 2023]

[179] J. J. Ratey, and E. M. Hallowell, *Driven to Distraction*, United States: Pantheon Books, 1994.

[180] S. Vanbuskirk, "When ADHD Is All in the Family: The upside of knowing that ADHD is highly heritable," *ADDitude*, [Online] https://www.additudemag.com/is-adhd-hereditary-blog/, April 8, 2022. [Accessed Jan. 26, 2023.]

[181] R. H. Bitsko, A. H. Claussen, J. Lichstein, *et al.*, "Mental health surveillance among children—United States, 2013–2019," *MMWR Suppl.*, Vol. 71, No. 2, pp. 1-48, 2022.

[182] S. Young, D. Moss, O. Sedgwick, M. Fridman, and P. Hodgkins, "A meta-analysis of the prevalence of attention deficit hyperactivity disorder in incarcerated populations," *Psychological Medicine*, Vol. 45, No. 2, pp. 247-258, 2015.

[183] S. Watson, "ADHD and Substance Abuse," *WebMD*, [Online] https://www.webmd.com/add-adhd/adhd-and-substance-abuse-is-there-a-link, Aug. 25, 2022. [Accessed Jan. 26, 2023.]

[184] D. Demontis, R. K. Walters, J. Martin, *et al.*, "Discovery of the first genome-wide significant risk loci for attention deficit/hyperactivity disorder," *Nat Genet*, Vol. 51, pp. 63–75, 2019.

[185] This technology was subsequently patented (Patent number 14/505262, "Systems and Methods for Composable Analytics") and licensed by an MIT Lincoln Laboratory spinoff called Composable Analytics, Inc. In full disclosure, I have received a small amount of royalties from that license. However, I have not followed the company and their products and services. This discussion neither represents the company's work nor endorses them, but I am proud of what those entrepreneurs have accomplished!

[186] Agile Alliance Editors, "Agile 101," *Agile Alliance*, https://www.agilealliance.org/agile101/, accessed Jan. 26, 2023.

[187] S. W. Ambler, "Answering the 'Where is the Proof That Agile Methods Work?' Question," *Ambysoft, Inc.*, http://www.agilemodeling.com/essays/proof.htm, accessed Jan 26, 2023.

CHAPTER 9 – INSTRUMENTS OF CHANGE

[188] N. Chomsky, *Understanding Power*, India: Penguin Group, pp. 139, 2003.

[189] Quest to Learn, "Research: Quest Learning Model Linked to Significant Learning Gains," https://www.q2l.org/about/research/, accessed Feb. 1, 2023.

[190] National Research Council, "Engaging Schools: Fostering High School Students' Motivation to Learn," Washington, DC: The National Academies Press, Vol. 18, 2003.

[191] Quest to Learn, https://www.q2l.org/about/, accessed Feb. 1, 2023.

[192] J. Shapiro, "What Happens When School Design Looks Like Game Design," *KQED*, [Online] https://www.kqed.org/mindshift/36814/what-happens-when-school-design-looks-like-game-design, July 24, 2014. [Accessed Feb. 1, 2023.]

[193] Quest to Learn, *InsideSchools*, https://insideschools.org/school/02M422, accessed Feb. 1, 2023.

[194] Public School Review, "Quest to Learn," https://www.publicschoolreview.com/quest-to-learn-profile, accessed Feb. 1, 2023.

[195] J. Dana, "The Utter Uselessness of Job Interviews," *New York Times*, [Online] https://www.nytimes.com/2017/04/08/opinion/sunday/the-utter-uselessness-of-job-interviews.html, April 8, 2017. [Accessed March 21, 2023.]

[196] C. Burdick, "The History of the Resume," *Davron*, [Online] https://www.davron.net/history-of-the-resume/, Feb. 10, 2016. [Accessed Jan. 30, 2023.]

[197] M. Russiello, "Does college GPA predict future job performance?," *HR Avatar*, [Online] https://www.hravatar.com/ta/blogs/43/hr-avatar-does-college-gpa-predict-future-job-performance.html, Jan. 20, 2016. [Accessed Jan. 30, 2023.]

[198] J. Hunter, and F. Schmidt, "Quantifying the effects of psychological interventions on employee job performance and work-force productivity," *American Psychologist*, Vol. 38, pp. 473-478, 1983. John Hunter's work is the most widely cited evidence for job performance correlation with various measures. However, those meta-analyses are decades old. I would expect the usefulness of GPA is even worse now given the clear GPA inflation of the past few decades.

[199] M. Ziegler, E. Dietl, M. Vogel, and M. Bühner, "Predicting Training Success with General Mental Ability, Specific Ability Tests, and (Un)Structured Interviews: A meta-analysis with unique samples," *Intl. Journal of Selection and Assessment*, Vol. 19, No. 2, pp. 170-182, 2011.

[200] N. Shpancer, "Poor Predictors: Job Interviews Are Useless and Unfair," *Psychology Today*, [Online] https://www.psychologytoday.com/us/blog/insight-therapy/202008/poor-predictors-job-interviews-are-useless-and-unfair, Aug. 31, 2020. [Accessed Jan. 30, 2023.]

[201] K. I. van der Zee, A. B. Bakker, and P. Bakker, "Why are structured interviews so rarely used in personnel selection?," *The Journal of applied psychology*, Vol. 87, No. 1, pp. 176–184, 2002.

[202] J. Levashina, C. J. Hartwell, F. P. Morgenson, and M. A. Campion, "The Structured Employment Interview: Narrative and Quantitative Review of the Research Literature," *Personnel Psychology*, Vol. 67, pp. 241-293, 2014.

[203] A. Pasick, "Google Finally Admits That Its Infamous Brainteasers Were Completely Useless for Hiring: 'A complete waste of time'," *The Atlantic*, [Online] https://www.theatlantic.com/business/archive/2013/06/google-finally-admits-that-its-infamous-brainteasers-were-completely-useless-for-hiring/277053/, June 20, 2013. [Accessed Jan. 30, 2023.]

[204] C. M. Berry, M. L. Gruys, and P. R. Sackett, "Educational attainment as a proxy for cognitive ability in selection: Effects on levels of cognitive ability and adverse impact," *Journal of Applied Psychology*, Vol. 91, No. 3, pp. 696–705, 2006.

[205] "Thomas Edison Test: Hiring Process," *Edison Innovation Foundation*, https://www.thomasedison.org/thomas-edison-hiring-test, accessed Jan. 30, 2023.

[206] K. Hagerty, "Google Foobar Challenge: Level 1," *Towards Data Science*, [Online] https://towardsdatascience.com/google-foobar-challenge-level-1-3487bb252780, July 5, 2022. [Accessed Jan. 30, 2023.]

[207] F. Kalman, "Gamification: Deloitte's leadership Learning Motivator," *Chief Learning Officer*, [Online] https://www.chieflearningofficer.com/2012/07/23/gamification-deloittes-leadership-learning-motivator/, July 13, 2012.

[208] S. Gupta, "Hack to hire: how hackathons can be tapped for recruitment needs," *YourStory*, [Online] https://yourstory.com/2020/05/hiring-hackathons-tap-recruitment-needs, May 25, 2020. [Accessed Jan. 30, 2023.]

[209] Airman Challenge, *U.S. Air Force*, https://www.airforce.com/airmanchallenge, accessed Jan. 30, 2023.

[210] N. Bika, "Gamification in recruiting: How and why to give it a shot," *Inside HR*, https://resources.workable.com/stories-and-insights/gamification-in-recruiting-effectiveness, accessed Jan. 30, 2023.

[211] D. Ravitch, "A Brief History of Testing and Accountability," *Hoover Institution*, [Online] https://www.hoover.org/research/brief-history-testing-and-accountability, Oct. 30, 2002. [Accessed Feb. 1, 2023.]

[212] J. S. Coleman, *Equality of Educational Opportunity*, United States: U.S. Department of Health, Education, and Welfare, Office of Education, 1966.

[213] B. O'Keefe, A. Rotherham, and J. O'Neal Schiess, "Reshaping Assessment and Accountability in 2021 and Beyond," *National Association of State Boards of Education*, https://files.eric.ed.gov/fulltext/EJ1315295.pdf, May 2001.

[214] Digest of Education Statistics, "Table 225.10. Average number of Carnegie units earned by public high school graduates in various subject fields, by sex and race/ethnicity: Selected years, 1982 through 2009," *National Center for Education Statistics*, https://nces.ed.gov/programs/digest/d16/tables/dt16_225.10.asp, accessed Feb. 1, 2023.

[215] S. D. Sparks, "Even before Pandemic, National Test Finds Most Seniors Unready for College Reading, Math," *Education Week*, [Online] https://www.edweek.org/teaching-learning/even-before-pandemic-national-test-finds-most-seniors-unready-for-college-reading-math/2020/10, October 28, 2020. [Accessed Feb. 1, 2023.]

[216] K. Salen, "Designing a Place Called School: A Case Study of the Public School Quest to Learn," *She Ji: The Journal of Design, Economics, and Innovation*, Vol. 3, No. 1, pp. 51-64, 2017.

[217] "Teacher Demographics and Statistics in the US," *Zippia: The Career Expert*, https://www.zippia.com/teacher-jobs/demographics/, accessed Jan. 31, 2023.

[218] J. Hattie, *Visible Learning: A Synthesis of Over 800 Meta-Analyses Relating to Achievement (1st ed.)*, Routledge, 2008.

[219] D.S. Ones, S. Dilchert, C. Viswesvaran, and J.F. Salgado, "Cognitive ability," In: *The Oxford handbook of Personnel assessment and selection*, N. Schmitt (Ed.), New York, NY: Oxford University Press, pp. 179-224, 2012.

[220] L. Bardach, and R. M. Klassen, "Smart teachers, successful students? A systematic review of the literature on teachers' cognitive abilities and teacher effectiveness," *Educational Research Review*, Vol. 30, 2020.

[221] C. T. Clotfelter, H. F. Ladd, and J. L. Vigdor, "How and Why do Teacher Credentials Matter for Student Achievement?," NBER Working Paper No. 12828, *National Bureau of Education Research*, http://www.nber.org/papers/w12828, Jan. 2007.

[222] OECD, *Education at a Glance 2022: OECD Indicators*, Paris: OECD Publishing, 2022.

[223] J. D. Agresti, and R. McCutcheon, "Education Facts," *Just Facts*, www.justfacts.com/education.asp, last modified January 3, 2023.

[224] S. Cavanagh, "K-12 Spending: Where the Money Goes," *EdWeek Market Brief*, [Online] https://marketbrief.edweek.org/marketplace-k-12/k-12-spending-where-the-money-goes/, Jun 1, 2017. [Accessed Feb. 1, 2023.]

[225] National Center for Education Statistics, *Digest of Education Statistics*, https://nces.ed.gov/programs/digest/d17/tables/dt17_211.60.asp, August 2017.

[226] National Center for Education Statistics, "Staff employed in public elementary and secondary school systems, by type of assignment: Selected years, 1949-50 through fall 2017," *Digest of Education Statistics*, Table 213.10, https://nces.ed.gov/programs/digest/d19/tables/dt19_213.10.asp, August 2019.

[227] D. H. Meadows, *Thinking in Systems: A Primer*, United Kingdom: Chelsea Green Pub., 2008

INDEX